The Best After-Dinner Stories

The Best
After-Dinner
Stories

Selected and introduced by
TIM HEALD
With illustrations by
PAUL COX

LONDON
The Folio Society
2003

TYPESET IN GALLIARD AT THE FOLIO SOCIETY
PRINTED IN GREAT BRITAIN AT THE BATH PRESS, BATH
ON BUHL WOVE PAPER AND BOUND BY THEM IN FULL
CLOTH PRINTED WITH A DESIGN BY THE ARTIST

Contents

6

Introduction

Being asked to 'be kind enough to say a few words after dinner' is a hazard of middle and old age. This is partly why, forty years after leaving school, I found myself addressing the Chartered Surveyors' Branch of my Old Boys' Association at the Royal Thames Yacht Club in London. It reminded me of the old joke, frequently adapted by after-dinner speakers, which I first heard fall from the lips of the silkily eloquent novelist Francis King when he rose, as International President of PEN, to speak after yet another gala dinner in Lugano. Francis told his audience that he had had a nightmare in which he dreamt that he was speaking to PEN delegates in Italy and woke up to find that he was. In my speech I naturally told the old boys that I had dreamt I was addressing the Old Shirburnian Chartered Surveyors – and, like Francis, and countless others before us – woke up to find that the dream wasn't a dream at all.

If, when you utter similar words, suitably adapted to your particular circumstances, you do not hear at least a ripple of laughter, then you are in trouble.

While jokes are indispensable to the after-dinner speaker, there is no such thing as an after-dinner entertainment that is all jokes. Proper stories and proper speeches have beginnings and middles and ends, though it isn't always easy to identify them. In an anthology it is proper to begin as near the beginning as possible, and to proceed through the middle to the end. In practice, after-dinner speeches are always pausing for comic asides, digressions, anecdotes and interruptions. It is going to be the same here. Really accomplished after-dinner speakers manage to turn down innumerable apparently blind alleys and culs-de-sac, emerging triumphantly only to dive down another one, taking their smiling audience with them, until they finally arrive at a peroration which has everyone on their feet stamping and cheering. Every word will appear to have tripped lightly off the tongue with never a moment of preparation, but in fact, of course, the speaker will have worked over it long and hard.

The consumption of food and drink as a social event, distinct from simple sustenance, has been going on for thousands of years. Changing for dinner, making conversation during the meal, the general social bonding associated with eating and drinking among friends are as old as bread and wine themselves. But at what point did the first host or toastmaster say, as the plates were cleaned and throats cleared, 'I'd like to call upon Mr so-and-so such-and-such to say a few words?'

The Bible is an obvious starting point but, although the Good Book is full of significant meals and meaningful stories, it's surprising how few occasions quite fit the bill. The miraculous business of the loaves and the fishes, when a bad case of under-catering was saved by divine intervention, was not followed by an after-dinner speech from Our Lord. In fact, while the leftovers were being gathered up into baskets he and the disciples made a speedy exit by boat without, as far as I can see, saying a word. The Last Supper contained some of the most memorable mealtime words ever uttered but they were delivered during and not after the meal. It was pretty sombre stuff too – not at all what is associated with after-dinner speaking in modern times.

Earlier still, of course, were the Greeks. In Book IX of Homer's *Odyssey* Odysseus stands up to speak after dinner and doesn't sit down again until four books later. At the start of Book XIII Homer reports: '. . . such was the spell he had cast on the whole company that not a sound was heard throughout the shadowy hall'. An impressive response to 17,000-odd lines.

Ideally, I would have liked to have been able to start with scenes in a cave somewhere as the assembled company wiped the last vestiges of mammoth juice from their chins. Alas, if some prehistoric graffiti does exist to record the first after-dinner oration, I haven't found it. I have begun, however, as near the beginning as possible, with Chaucer's pilgrims in the Tabard Inn, cantering briskly through the rather male-dominated dinners of history before arriving with some relief at the sexually emancipated present day.

At the back of my mind throughout was the salutary lesson learned when consulting the net in preparation for a speech of my own. I tapped 'after-dinner speeches' into the search engine 'Google dot com' and it threw up no less than 77,900 entries – and extremely depressing most of them were.

There were, for example, dogmatic entries from American universities of which I had not previously heard. One typical item, put out by the Faculty of 'Speech and Debate' somewhere in the mid-west, was headed: 'Event Category: Public Address. Time Limit: Ten minutes. Delivery Style: Memorized.' The key paragraph went: 'The speech may be either informative or persuasive in nature. It is important to remember, however, that every ADS must have a serious thesis (informative or persuasive) and cannot merely represent "stand-up" comedy. After-dinner speeches must contain all of the elements of good public speeches. Humour in after-dinner speaking should be in good taste and the speaker should keep his or her audience in mind when devising jokes, puns and one-liners. Multiple sources should be used and cited during the speech. Minimal notes are permitted, but memorized delivery is preferred.'

Just to emphasise a certain sort of academic's ability to take the fun out of anything, this entry concluded: 'Deviations from the prescribed time limit should be punished according to the severity of the infraction.' I was reminded of the after-dinner speaker who went on and on until a guest was so fed up that he picked up a bottle and shied it at the speaker's head. Unfortunately it missed the speaker and hit a

little man sitting beside him, knocking him out. Immediately people rushed to revive him, and when he eventually
came round, he was heard to say: 'Please hit me again. I can
still hear him.'

Speaking recently on board a Mediterranean cruise ship, I
invited my audience to provide me with some suitable after-
dinner stories for this book. One of my colleagues, John
Garnon-Williams, responded with a military story about a
visiting lecturer from Oxford who was, somewhat improbably, called upon to address some squaddies on the subject
of the poet Keats. He was introduced by the Regimental
Sergeant-Major, who said, 'This is Professor Jones who is
going to speak to you horrible, dozy little men about Keats.
Now some of you are so bloody ignorant you don't even
know what a keat is, so listen well.'

I remember another story told by John Bromley. Bromley, who died in 2002, was a broadcaster of note, a pillar of
the Lord's Taverners and a much loved after-dinner speaker.
His favourite story, without which none of his speeches was
complete, concerned a pub lunch. The sign outside the pub
says, 'Come in for a pint, a pie and a friendly word.' The
weary traveller pulls in, enters the pub and orders the pint
and the pie. When he has taken his first sip of beer he says to
the barman, 'Now, what about the friendly word?'; whereupon the barman leans forward with a confidential air and
says, 'Don't eat the pie.'

There may be moments in this book, ladies and gentlemen, when you might feel like offering such a friendly word
to your neighbour. Tastes vary, of course, and after-dinner
speaking is a subjective business. One man's jokes are
another man's yawns. There will always be someone in the
room who doesn't see the point or get the joke. Sometimes
that may be the speaker himself. But I hope that for the
most part you will agree that, where I have put in a finger, I
have pulled out a plum.

My Lords, Ladies and Gentlemen . . .

THE SCENE IS THE TABARD INN, SOUTHWARK, in fourteenth-century England. The occasion is the beginning of a pilgrimage to Thomas Becket's shrine in Canterbury. The pilgrims have clearly had plenty to eat and are in mellow mood after dinner when the innkeeper decides that, er, a few words would be in order and rises to his feet. He addresses them in exactly the spirit of jovial challenge appropriate to the occasion – no jokes as we understand them, but a high level of entertainment, wit and raillery. *The Canterbury Tales* are among the most famous after-dinner stories in the English language, so this seems an excellent place to start: ladies and gentlemen, pray silence for mine host of the Tabard Inn, as reported by Geoffrey Chaucer.

Our host

Our host gave each and all a warm welcome,
And set us down to supper there and then.
The eatables he served were of the best;
Strong was the wine; we matched it with our thirst.
A handsome man OUR HOST, handsome indeed,
And a fit master of ceremonies.
He was a big man with protruding eyes
– You'll find no better burgess in Cheapside –
Racy in talk, well-schooled and shrewd was he;
Also a proper man in every way.
And moreover he was a right good sort,
And after supper he began to joke,
And, when we had all paid our reckonings,
He spoke of pleasure, among other things:
'Truly,' said he, 'ladies and gentlemen,
Here you are all most heartily welcome.
Upon my word – I'm telling you no lie –
All year I've seen no jollier company
At one time in this inn than I have now.
I'd make some fun for you, if I knew how.

And, as it happens, I have just now thought
Of something that will please you, at no cost.
'You're off to Canterbury – so Godspeed!
The blessed martyr give you your reward!
And I'll be bound, that while you're on your way,
You'll be telling tales, and making holiday;
It makes no sense, and really it's no fun
To ride along the road dumb as a stone.
And therefore I'll devise a game for you,
To give you pleasure, as I said I'd do.
And if with one accord you all consent
To abide by my decision and judgement,
And if you'll do exactly as I say,
Tomorrow, when you're riding on your way,
Then, by my father's soul – for he is dead –
If you don't find it fun, why, here's my head!
Now not another word! Hold up your hands!'
We were not long in making up our minds.
It seemed not worth deliberating, so
We gave our consent without more ado,
Told him to give us what commands he wished.
'Ladies and gentlemen,' began our host,
'Do yourselves a good turn, and hear me out:
But please don't turn your noses up at it.
I'll put it in a nutshell: here's the nub:
It's that you each, to shorten the long journey,
Shall tell two tales *en route* to Canterbury,
And, coming homeward, tell another two,
Stories of things that happened long ago.
Whoever best acquits himself, and tells
The most amusing and instructive tale,
Shall have a dinner, paid for by us all,
Here in this inn, and under this roof-tree,
When we come back again from Canterbury.
To make it the more fun, I'll gladly ride
With you at my own cost, and be your guide.

And anyone who disputes what I say
Must pay all our expenses on the way!
And if this plan appeals to all of you,
Tell me at once, and with no more ado,
And I'll make my arrangements here and now.'
    To this we all agreed, and gladly swore
To keep our promises; and furthermore
We asked him if he would consent to do
As he had said, and come and be our leader,
And judge our tales, and act as arbiter,
Set up our dinner too at a fixed price;
And we'd obey whatever he might decide
In everything. And so, with one consent,
We bound ourselves to bow to his judgement.
And thereupon wine was at once brought in.
We drank; and not long after, everyone
Went off to bed, and that without delay.

Geoffrey Chaucer

One can't include Chaucer and omit Shakespeare, which, like the Bible, is full of food and drink and some amazingly memorable dinners. Most of the action, however, takes place actually during the meals, with such pièces de résistance as the sudden appearance of Banquo's ghost when the Macbeths are at table. 'What bloody man is that?' asks Lady Macbeth – a question which has since been asked around a million such tables as the Unknown Speaker stumbles to his feet in answer to the toastmaster's summons.

    The most memorable piece of post-prandialism in Shakespeare is similar to the host's challenge at the opening of *The Canterbury Tales*. This is when Henry V, geeing up his troops before the Battle of Agincourt, tells them that when

they get home they have to hold an annual anniversary dinner at which they will get up and brag about their derring-
do on the field of battle. He doesn't say anything about
jokes or even funny stories but he does suggest a high
degree of showing off. This is something common to all
the best after-dinner storytellers. Basil Boothroyd, one of
the classic late twentieth-century after-dinner yarn-spinners,
actually invented an organisation called GADSKIS – the
Guild of After Dinner Speakers and Kindred Insufferable
Show-Offs.

King Henry clearly expects the survivors of Agincourt to
be fully paid-up members of GADSKIS. He begins by ques-
tioning how his cousin Warwick could even think of wishing
for more soldiers when these would detract from their own
glory.

Henry V's St Crispin's Day speech

What's he that wishes so?
My cousin Warwick? No, my fair cousin.
If we are marked to die, we are enough
To do our country loss; and if to live,
The fewer men, the greater share of honour.
God's will, I pray thee wish not one man more.
By Jove, I am not covetous for gold,
Nor care I who doth feed upon my cost;
It ernes me not if men my garments wear;
Such outward things dwell not in my desires.
But if it be a sin to covet honour
I am the most offending soul alive.
No, faith, my coz, wish not a man from England.
God's peace, I would not lose so great an honour
As one man more methinks would share from me
For the best hope I have. O do not wish one more.
Rather proclaim it presently through my host
That he which hath no stomach to this fight,
Let him depart. His passport shall be made
And crowns for convoy put into his purse.
We would not die in that man's company
That fears his fellowship to die with us.
This day is called the Feast of Crispian.
He that outlives this day and comes safe home
Will stand a-tiptoe when this day is named
And rouse him at the name of Crispian.
He that shall see this day and live t'old age
Will yearly on the vigil feast his neighbours
And say, 'Tomorrow is Saint Crispian.'
Then will he strip his sleeve and show his scars
And say, 'These wounds I had on Crispin's day.'
Old men forget; yet all shall be forgot,
But he'll remember, with advantages,
What feats he did that day. Then shall our names,

William Shakespeare

Familiar in his mouth as household words –
Harry the King, Bedford and Exeter,
Warwick and Talbot, Salisbury and Gloucester –
Be in their flowing cups freshly remember'd.
This story shall the good man teach his son,
And Crispin Crispian shall ne'er go by
From this day to the ending of the world
But we in it shall be remember'd,
We few, we happy few, we band of brothers.
For he today that sheds his blood with me
Shall be my brother; be he ne'er so vile,
This day shall gentle his condition.
And gentlemen in England now abed
Shall think themselves accursed they were not here,
And hold their manhood cheap whiles any speaks
That fought with us upon Saint Crispin's day.

Stirring stuff, but, as William Makepeace Thackeray pointed out several centuries later, using the Battle of Waterloo as an example, such bragging can have the opposite effect.

Waterloo

It is, my dear, the happy privilege of your sex in England to quit the dinner-table after the wine-bottles have once or twice gone round it, and you are thereby saved (though, to be sure, I can't tell what the ladies do upstairs) – you are saved two or three hours' excessive dulness, which the men are obliged to go through.

I ask any gentleman who reads this to remember espe-cially how many times, how many hundred times, how many

thousand times, in his hearing, the battle of Waterloo has been discussed after dinner, and to call to mind how cruelly he has been bored by the discussion. 'Ah, it was lucky for us that the Prussians came up!' says one little gentleman, looking particularly wise and ominous. 'Hang the Prussians!' (or, perhaps, something stronger 'the Prussians!') says a stout old major on half-pay. 'We beat the French without them, sir, as beaten them we always have! We were thundering down the hill of Belle Alliance, sir, at the backs of them, and the French were crying "Sauve qui peut" long before the Prussians ever touched them!' And so the battle opens, and for many mortal hours, amid rounds of claret, rages over and over again.

I thought to myself, considering the above things, what a fine thing it will be in after-days to say that I have been to Brussels and never seen the field of Waterloo; indeed, that I am such a philosopher as not to care a fig about the battle – nay, to regret, rather, that when Napoleon came back, the British Government had not spared their men and left him alone.

But this pitch of philosophy was unattainable. This morning, after having seen the Park, the fashionable boulevard, the pictures, the cafés – having sipped, I say, the sweets of every flower that grows in this paradise of Brussels, quite weary of the place, we mounted on a Namur diligence, and jingled off at four miles an hour for Waterloo . . .

. . . English glory does not condescend to ask the names of the poor devils whom she kills in her service. Why was not every private man's name written upon the stones in Waterloo Church as well as every officer's? Five hundred pounds to the stone-cutters would have served to carve the whole catalogue, and paid the poor compliment of recognition to men who died in doing their duty. If the officers deserved a stone, the men did. But come, let us away and drop a tear over the Marquis of Anglesey's leg!

As for Waterloo, has it not been talked of enough after dinner? Here are some oats that were plucked before Hougoumont, where grow not only oats, but flourishing crops of grape-shot, bayonets, and legion-of-honour crosses, in amazing profusion.

Well, though I made a vow not to talk about Waterloo either here or after dinner, there is one little secret admission that one must make after seeing it. Let an Englishman go and see that field, and he *never forgets it*. The sight is an event in his life; and though it has been seen by millions of peaceable *gents* – grocers from Bond Street, meek attorneys from Chancery Lane, and timid tailors from Piccadilly – I will wager that there is not one of them but feels a glow as he looks at the place, and remembers that he, too, is an Englishman.

It is a wrong, egotistical, savage, unchristian feeling, and that's the truth of it. A man of peace has no right to be dazzled by that red-coated glory, and to intoxicate his vanity with those remembrances of carnage and triumph. The same sentence which tells us that on earth there ought to be peace and good-will amongst men, tells us to whom GLORY belongs.

William Makepeace Thackeray

22

The man most famous for his dinner-table talk emerged on the scene a couple of hundred years after Shakespeare, although most of his most famous stories were, like those in the Bible, actually uttered during rather than after meals. Not for Dr Johnson – for it is he – the anxious after-dinner break, sitting on the loo scribbling notes on the carefully prepared speech, feeling slightly sick and wishing one were at home with a good book and a mug of Ovaltine. He was up and running before the first slurp of soup, ladies and gentlemen. And, just as much to the point, his amanuensis Boswell had his pen and notebook out before they'd even sat down to dine.

But when it came to table talk, he was a hundred-metre man rather than a long-distance runner. Classic one-liners abound but none of your weighty two- or three-hour Victorian jobs or even your twenty-first-century ten-minute

sparklers. 'I have, sir, neither the patience nor the inclination,' he would have said, shovelling down another oyster
and gulping at his claret. 'A story after dinner is a tale without legs.' Well something like that. Here, then, is Boswell's
Johnson, as paraphrased by another witty after-dinnerist,
A. P. Herbert (of whom more later).

In brief

A man is in general better pleased when he has a good dinner on his table than when he has a wife who talks Greek.

On playing the violin: Difficult, do you call it, Sir? I wish it
were impossible.

On money-making: There are few ways in which a man can
be more innocently employed than in getting money.

Of a female writer: She is better employed at her toilet than
using her pen; better reddening her own cheeks than black-
ening others' characters.

On terminological inexactitudes: Boswell: Suppose, Sir, we
believe one half of what he tells us? Johnson: Aye, Sir, but
we do not know which half to believe.

Of Scotland: Johnson: That is a very foul country, to be
sure. Boswell: Well, Sir, God made it. Johnson: Certainly
He did. But you must always remember He made it for
Scotsmen.

The Irish are a fair people. They never speak well of one
another.

Samuel Johnson

Dr Johnson would certainly have had to reconsider his attitude to women if he had ever come across Libby Purves, the author, broadcaster and journalist, who, in her inaugural speech as president of Johnson's very own Society – accompanied by steak and kidney pudding and the smoking of clay pipes – acknowledged the paradoxical nature of her position.

Address to the Samuel Johnson Society

Good evening. Since I believe it is over twenty years since your last woman president, I feel it is my job to remind you of the one Johnson saying that every member of this Society has been far too tactful to quote today: the one about a woman's preaching being like a dog walking on its hinder legs – it is not done well, but we are surprised to see it done at all.

It's a strange position to be in, taking on this honour: on the one hand I feel entirely at home, since a great many of the remarks and views of Samuel Johnson have been part of the casual furniture of my mind for some thirty years now, ever since school. On the other hand I know perfectly well that there's very little I can say to you about Dr Johnson that you haven't already thought or heard before. I feel very humbly aware that this society has had among its presidents many real scholars; and that I am not one of them.

I *was* once the embryo of a scholar – as an undergraduate at St Anne's, Oxford – and indeed one of my favourite subjects always was Dr Johnson; which says a lot for him, because I heartily disliked just about all his contemporaries – if it were not for him my tastes would have gone straight from the seventeenth-century Metaphysicals to the Romantics, with no intervening Augustans at all. My God, how I have suffered from Dryden! But never mind. I left Oxford without progressing to postgraduate studies, because I discovered in a rare moment of accurate self-knowledge that while I enjoyed reading for my weekly essay, and enjoyed writing it, what I enjoyed even more was reading it out, with extravagant gestures, at the tutorial. Showbiz kept edging into scholarship; rather as in the case of Johnson's subject who wanted to be a philosopher, but 'cheerfulness was always breaking in'.

So it had to be Grub Street. The modern Grub Street, not quite so harsh as Samuel Johnson's but with the same essential elements of journalism: overstatement, argument, polemic, attention-grabbing and a kind of wild exhibitionist sincerity. But with this rejected ambition behind me, at least I am ever aware of the contrast between what a hack does and says, and what a scholar does and says. Believe it or not, we hacks and columnists and commentators do, quite often, recognise our limits: the limits imposed by deadlines, and insufficient time for research, and the need to be a general-ist, not a specialist; and the fact that we write today for tomorrow, and are buffeted by gales of changing opinion and the exhilaration of debate.

So the Samuel Johnson I celebrate today is not quite, not yet in his life, Dr Johnson, the respected lexicographer with faithful Boswell at his heels. For most of his life he too lived in the hacks' world. His formal studies were curtailed not by personal choice but by poverty and illness. So he became an 'adventurer in literature', and wrote for *The Gentleman's Magazine* – anything he could – odes and epigrams, epi-taphs and reviews and pocket Lives. He also, of course, wrote his wildly creative and highly partisan parliamentary reports. Years later, listening to praise being poured on a famous speech by Pitt the Elder, he broke in: 'Gentlemen, that speech I wrote in a garret in Exeter Street.' That young Johnson lived in a world of hackwork and bluff, doing his best, but above all doing it for the money. The eminent Johnson, once his name was made, retained that journalistic breeziness and gave us a host of defiant defences of it. 'No man but a blockhead ever wrote, except for money,' he said; and when challenged on why he got something wrong in the Dictionary, 'Ignorance, madam, pure ignorance.' Then there was the famous excuse for not printing the names of subscribers in his Dictionary – he said that there were two good reasons for this, that he had lost all the names, and that he had spent all the money.

The Johnson I love lived in two worlds; his innate high seriousness forever balanced by the defiant frivolity of the hack. He revelled in wit and paradox – although his tormented mind only reposed, as he said, on the security of truth. He was by nature a man of agonised religious feeling, but he couldn't resist a joke: even in the heart of the Dictionary, which was his one great throw for literary fame and respectability, there are famous jokes. ('Lexicographer: a harmless drudge' – and the joke about oats and Scotsmen, too hackneyed to repeat.) He was every inch the journalist: although he believed in hard drudging work – perspiration serving inspiration – he still managed never to get up before noon unless he had to.

But again the paradox: although he had to drag himself to work, he loathed the pretensions of rich and temperamental poets, with their bursts of inspiration and their callings on the Muse. 'A man may write at any time if he will only set himself doggedly to it,' he said firmly; and 'What is written without effort is generally read without pleasure.' Again and again he insisted that writers like himself are not geniuses or prophets, but just dogged spirits who 'have seldom any claim to the trade of writing, but that they have tried some other without success. They perceive no particular summons to composition except the sound of the clock . . . and about the opinion of posterity they have little solicitude, for their productions are seldom intended to remain in the world longer than a week.'

More poignantly, in the preface to the Dictionary, he said it all for the unsupported scholar, the hack without means, who would in his guilty heart like to do something solid, but who must do it to a deadline or starve:

'In this work,' he wrote, 'when it shall be found that much is omitted, let it not be forgotten that much likewise is performed. And though no book was ever spared out of tenderness to the author, and the world is little solicitous to know whence proceeded the faults of that which it con-demns – yet it may gratify curiosity to inform it, that the English Dictionary was written with little assistance of the learned, and without any patronage of the great; not in the soft obscurities of retirement, or under the shelter of academick bowers, but amidst inconvenience and distrac-tion, in sickness and in sorrow.'

His wife had died, his dear Tetty. And it was not for another seven years after the Dictionary was published and acclaimed that he was delivered from the anxiety of writing for bread. George III gave him a pension of £300 a year. Even so he regarded it as an embarrassment to an honest man until the Prime Minister, Lord Bute, reassured him that the money 'is not given for anything you are to do – but for what you have done'. So he took it, and at last – for the first time ever – enjoyed some security.

All these things you already know: I repeat them like this to underline why paid writers, insecure writers, freelance journalists for two centuries have loved the man. And not just us; freelance actors, too, who remember how he mourned Garrick's death as 'eclipsing the gaiety of nations and the world's stock of innocent enjoyment'. The last time I spent a whole evening talking about Johnson was when I was sent – myself a hack – to the location of Robbie Col-trane and John Sessions' dramatised version of Johnson and Boswell's *Tour of the Hebrides*. I found them up a hillside in Mull, in the drizzling rain, filming a scene where Johnson takes a lift on a farm-cart and Boswell falls off. As is usual in these situations, the producers possibly told me that I would be allowed 'half an hour maximum' to do a brief interview with the stars after dinner, because they had lines to learn. In the event, I found that Robbie Coltrane and John Sessions

are both genuine, passionate Johnsonians, and we began firing off anecdotes and lines at one another all through dinnertime: his heartfelt words on liberty, his peerless sarcasm, his jokes, his private charities, his devastating critical barbs, his kindness, his worldliness, his pugnacity. As Oliver Goldsmith fondly said, there was 'no arguing with Johnson – when his pistol misses fire he knocks you down with the butt of it'.

We were all at it, the three of us, passionately remembering this single figure of two centuries before – over a disgraceful amount of whisky – until two o'clock in the morning. I do not know whether they ever learnt their lines that night, but I had some trouble finding my way out of bed the next morning and onto the mainland ferry . . .

Libby Purves

Ladies and gentlemen, I apologise for that digression. We are running ahead of ourselves. Ms Purves is happily still with us in the twenty-first century and we should still be in the eighteenth century, listening to that memorable Member of Parliament, Charles Townshend.

My attention was drawn to one of his speeches by my former history teacher, Derek Jarrett, who ran the School Debating Society at Sherborne. There he tried to teach one the first principles of speaking in public, the best of which was always to prepare properly. Most audiences will forgive anything if they think the speaker has made an effort. No audience appreciates the feeling that they're getting a rag-bag of old jokes no matter how funny or deftly delivered. Anyway, Derek remarked that 'the eighteenth-century cus-tom of dining in the middle of the afternoon, with the passing of the port a separate episode after the ladies had left, probably discouraged the preparation of formal after-dinner speeches.'

This being so, Derek, who edited the whole of Horace Walpole's œuvre for Yale University Press, fell back on the famous speech Townshend delivered while under the influ-ence of drink – or at least of champagne, which is frequently regarded as not an alcoholic beverage in the accepted sense ('Champagne for my real friends, real pain for my sham friends', as the famous old toast goes). Whether Towns-hend's speech was as coruscating as everyone thought is open to question. As with Johnson and so many after-dinner specialists, the speech would have disappeared into thin air had it not been reported by a gifted listener who may have tweaked it up a bit. Where Johnson had Boswell, Towns-hend, on this occasion at least, had Horace Walpole. What Townshend actually said after dinner may not have been particularly wonderful, but what Walpole said he said is a classic. It may not quite fit the precise definition of 'after-dinner speech' but, as Derek Jarrett says, 'it was at least delivered after he had dined, even though the people who listened to it were not the diners'. And in Walpole's hand it makes a great story, if rather a tall one.

Charles Townshend's champagne speech

It was on that day and on that occasion that Charles Townshend displayed in a latitude beyond belief the amazing powers of his capacity, and the no less amazing incongruities of his character. He had taken on himself early in the day, the examination of the Company's conduct; and in a very cool sensible speech on that occasion, and with a becoming consciousness of his own levity, had told the House, that he hoped he had atoned for the inconsideration of his past life by the care he had taken of that business. He had scarce uttered this speech, but, as if to atone for that (however false) atonement, he left the House, and went home to dinner, not concerning himself with Dyson's motion that was to follow. As that motion was however of a novel nature, it produced suspicion, objection and difficulties. Conway being pressed, and not caring to be the sole champion of an invidious measure, that was in reality not only in Townshend's province, but which he had had a principal hand in framing, sent for him back to the House. He returned about eight in the evening half drunk with champagne, and more intoxicated with spirits. He rose to speak without giving himself time to learn, and without caring what had been in agitation, except that the motion had given an alarm. The first thing he did, was to call God to witness that he had not been consulted on the motion – a confession implying that he was not consulted on a business in his own department; and the more marvellous, as the disgrace, of which he seemed to complain or boast of, was absolutely false. There were sitting round him twelve persons who had been in consultation with him that very morning and with his assistance had drawn up the motion on his own table, and who were petrified at his most unparalleled effrontery and causeless

want of truth. When he sat down again, Conway asked him
softly how he could affirm so gross a falsehood? he replied
carelessly 'I thought it would be better to say so' – but
before he sat down, he had poured forth such a torrent of
wit, parts, humour, knowledge, absurdity, vanity and fiction,
heightened by all the graces of comedy, the happiness of
allusion and quotation, and the buffoonery of farce. To the
purpose of the question he said not a syllable. It was a des-
cant on the times, a picture of parties, of their leaders, of
their hopes and defects. It was an encomium and a satire on
himself; and while he painted the pretensions of birth,
riches, connections, favour, titles, while he affected to praise
Lord Rockingham, and that faction, and yet insinuated that
nothing but parts like his own were qualified to preside; and
while he less covertly arraigned the wild incapacity of Lord
Chatham; he excited such murmurs of wonder, admiration,
applause, laughter, pity and scorn, that nothing was so true
as the sentence with which he concluded, when speaking of
government, he said, it was become what he himself had
often been called, a weathercock.
    Such was the wit, abundance, and impropriety of this

speech, that for some days men could talk or inquire of nothing else. 'Did you hear Charles Townshend's champagne speech?' was the universal question. For myself, I protest it was the most singular pleasure of the kind I ever tasted. The bacchanalian enthusiasm of Pindar flowed in torrents less rapid and less eloquent, and inspires less delight than Townshend's imagery, which conveyed meaning in every sentence. It was Garrick writing and acting extempore scenes of Congreve. A light circumstance increased the mirth of the audience. In the fervour of speaking Townshend rubbed off the patch from his eye, which he had represented as grievously cut three days before: no mark was discernible, but to the nearest spectators a scratch so slight, that he might have made, and perhaps had made, it himself, with a pin. To me the entertainment of the day was complete. He went to supper with us at Mr Conway's, where, the flood of his gaiety not being exhausted, he kept the table on a roar till two in the morning, by various sallies and pictures, the last of which was a scene in which he mimicked inimitably his own wife and another great lady, with whom he fancied himself in love, and both whose foibles and manner he counterfeited to the life. Mere lassitude closed his lips at last, not the want of wit and new ideas.

Horace Walpole

Speaking after drinking is a hazardous undertaking but some of the great set pieces in comic literature are the stories of what happened when the speaker was drunk. P. G. Wodehouse had a good line on booze. 'It was my Uncle George who discovered that alcohol was a food well in advance of modern medical thought,' he wrote in *The Inimitable Jeeves*. This view is widely shared by other characters in the Master's work. Jeeves himself had a 'pick-me-up'

which was guaranteed to produce results 'in anything short of an Egyptian mummy'. The Wodehouse world is full of 'excellent browsing and sluicing and cheery conversation'. This is all very well but not always the best prelude to standing up in front of an expectant audience and saying the proverbial few words – as poor old Gussie Finknottle found. What happened to Gussie when he had a jar too far before venturing forth on a formal speech is, ladies and gentlemen, one of the great cautionary tales of the English language – not technically an after-dinner story but a classic after-drinks story, which nearly always comes to much the same thing.

A few auspicious words

'Today,' said the bearded bloke, 'we are all happy to welcome as the guest of the afternoon Mr Fitz-Wattle –'

At the beginning of the address, Gussie had subsided into a sort of daydream, with his mouth hanging open. About halfway through, faint signs of life had begun to show. And for the last few minutes he had been trying to cross one leg over the other and failing and having another shot and failing again. But only now did he exhibit any real animation. He sat up with a jerk.

'Fink-Nottle,' he said, opening his eyes.

'Fitz-Nottle.'

'Fink-Nottle.'

'I should say Fink-Nottle.'

'Of course you should, you silly ass,' said Gussie genially.

'All right, get on with it.'

And closing his eyes, he began trying to cross his legs again.

I could see that this little spot of friction had rattled the bearded bloke a bit. He stood for a moment fumbling at the fungus with a hesitating hand. But they make these headmasters of tough stuff. The weakness passed. He came back nicely and carried on.

'We are all happy, I say, to welcome as the guest of the afternoon Mr Fink-Nottle, who has kindly consented to award the prizes. This task, as you know, is one that should have devolved upon that well-beloved and vigorous member of our board of governors, the Rev. William Plomer, and we are all, I am sure, very sorry that illness at the last moment should have prevented him from being here today. But, if I may borrow a familiar metaphor from the – if I may employ a homely metaphor familiar to you all – what we lose on the swings we gain on the roundabouts.'

He paused, and beamed rather freely, to show that this was comedy. I could have told the man it was no use. Not a ripple. The corn chandler leaned against me and muttered 'Whoddidesay?' but that was all.

It's always a nasty jar to wait for the laugh and find that the gag hasn't got across. The bearded bloke was visibly discomposed. At that, however, I think he would have got by, had he not, at this juncture, unfortunately stirred Gussie up again.

'In other words, though deprived of Mr Plomer, we have with us this afternoon Mr Fink-Nottle. I am sure that Mr Fink-Nottle's name is one that needs no introduction to you. It is, I venture to assert, a name that is familiar to us all.'

'Not to you,' said Gussie.

And the next moment I saw what Jeeves had meant when he had described him as laughing heartily. 'Heartily' was absolutely the *mot juste*. It sounded like a gas explosion.

'You didn't seem to know it so dashed well, what, what?' said Gussie. And, reminded apparently by the word 'what' of the word 'Wattle', he repeated the latter some sixteen times with a rising inflection.

'Wattle, Wattle, Wattle,' he concluded. 'Right ho. Push on.'

But the bearded bloke had shot his bolt. He stood there, licked at last; and, watching him closely, I could see that he was now at the crossroads. I could spot what he was think-ing as clearly as if he had confided it to my personal ear. He wanted to sit down and call it a day, I mean, but the thought that gave him pause was that, if he did, he must then either uncork Gussie or take the Fink-Nottle speech as read and get straight on to the actual prize-giving.

It was a dashed tricky thing, of course, to have to decide on the spur of the moment. I was reading in the paper the other day about those birds who are trying to split the atom, the nub being that they haven't the foggiest as to what will happen if they do. It may be all right. On the other hand, it may not be all right. And pretty silly a chap would feel, no doubt, if, having split the atom, he suddenly found the house going up in smoke and himself torn limb from limb.

So with the bearded bloke. Whether he was abreast of the inside facts in Gussie's case, I don't know, but it was obvious to him by this time that he had run into something pretty hot. Trial gallops had shown that Gussie had his own way of doing things. Those interruptions had been enough to prove to the perspicacious that here, seated on the plat-form at the big binge of the season, was one who, if pushed forward to make a speech, might let himself go in a rather epoch-making manner.

On the other hand, chain him up and put a green-baize cloth over him, and where were you? The proceedings would be over about half an hour too soon.

It was, as I say, a difficult problem to have to solve, and, left to himself, I don't know what conclusion he would have come to. Personally, I think he would have played it safe. As it happened, however, the thing was taken out of his hands, for at this moment, Gussie, having stretched his arms and yawned a bit, switched on that pebble-beached smile again and tacked down to the edge of the platform.

'Speech,' he said affably.

He then stood with his thumbs in the armholes of his waistcoat, waiting for the applause to die down.

It was some time before this happened, for he had got a very fine hand indeed. I suppose it wasn't often that the boys of Market Snodsbury Grammar School came across a man public-spirited enough to call their headmaster a silly ass, and they showed their appreciation in no uncertain manner. Gussie may have been one over the eight, but as far as the majority of those present were concerned he was sitting on top of the world.

'Boys,' said Gussie, 'I mean ladies and gentlemen and boys, I do not detain you long, but I suppose on this occasion to feel compelled to say a few auspicious words. Ladies – and boys and gentlemen – we have all listened with interest to the remarks of our friend here who forgot to shave this morning – I don't know his name, but then he didn't know mine – Fitz-Wattle, I mean, absolutely absurd – which squares things up a bit – and we are all sorry that the Reverend What-ever-he-was-called should be dying of adenoids, but after all, here today, gone tomorrow, and all flesh is as grass, and what not, but that wasn't what I wanted to say. What I wanted to say was this – and I say it confidently – without fear of contradiction – I say, in short, I am happy to be here on this auspicious occasion and I take much pleasure in kindly awarding the prizes, consisting of the handsome books you see laid out on that table. As Shakespeare says, there are sermons in books, stones in the running brooks, or, rather, the other way about, and there you have it in a nutshell.'

It went well, and I wasn't surprised. I couldn't quite fol-low some of it, but anybody could see that it was real ripe stuff, and I was amazed that even the course of treatment he had been taking could have rendered so normally tongue-tied a dumb brick as Gussie capable of it.

It just shows, what any Member of Parliament will tell you, that if you want real oratory, the preliminary noggin is essential. Unless pie-eyed, you cannot hope to grip.

Perhaps it would be as well to leave him at this point . . . The inebriated misfortunes of Gussie Finknottle are fictional but there are, alas, many true stories involving drink and dinner. Sir Hugh Casson, himself an after-dinner story-teller of note, had at least one distressing example from his days as President of the Royal Academy.

Hugh Casson and Laurie Lee

Hugh Casson's last Royal Academy Dinner before his retirement in 1984 was a fraught event. This time the principal guests were the Prince and Princess of Wales, whose presence was obviously an acknowledgement of the affection they, particularly the Prince, felt for him. The main speaker, at Casson's own invitation, was Laurie Lee, who was an old friend from the days when Lee had worked on the Festival of Britain and who Casson knew was an amusing speaker. Or could be. On this occasion, Laurie Lee, beset by nerves, had unfortunately primed himself with a few drinks before the occasion began, enjoyed the Academy's excellent wines during the dinner, and had eaten nothing. Casson spotted the ominous signs of imminent disaster, and warned the Princess of Wales, who sat next to Laurie Lee, to keep an eye on him and if he began to ramble on to tell him to sit down. This was not Casson at his most sensitive, especially as Diana, still relatively unused to formal and what seemed to her very highbrow occasions, had already confessed to him her own nervousness at sitting next to a poet. However, all went well at first. Laurie Lee started in great form and was greeted with responsive laughter by the other diners, many of whom knew him well. Unfortunately, in a haze of bibulous euphoria, he then became over-confident, flung down his manuscript and started to extemporise. He seemed unstoppable. What he was saying made increasingly little sense and his audience was torn between laughter and embarrassment, between consternation that this should be happening in the heartland

39

of the establishment, and delight at being witnesses to such an uproarious episode. Eventually Diana, who was trying to suppress her own laughter, kicked Lee's shin, pulled at his jacket and managed to halt the flow of the speaker's rambling discourse. He sat down, left after a short while, and the evening resumed its traditional and stately course. Belatedly aware of his blunder, Lee then crossed the road to Green Park and lay in a heap on the grass, reduced to a state of misery and self-loathing.

Some might have resented this marring of a great occasion with its Royal guests and, for Hugh, such strong personal significance. But as another Academician pointed out, Hugh knew Laurie Lee well enough to have been aware of the risks involved in inviting him to speak, and this time the risk did not pay off. Afterwards, he simply felt terribly sorry for his friend, blamed himself a little, and generally played down the event as of little consequence. But, in all its

grandeur, all its laughter, all its demonstration of human frailty, it became a vivid memory for those who were present.

Jose Manser

Presiding over Laurie Lee giving an inebriated speech was, however, marginally less fraught than having the then Prime Minister, Margaret Thatcher, in the audience for one of his own . . .

A Thatcher put-down

Casson's fund of private stories was much enhanced by one about Margaret Thatcher's attendance at an Academy dinner, where she arrived, regal and radiant, in a black taffeta dress. For a Socialist voter he reacted with surprising sympathy to her confession that there had been little exposure to the arts in 'the primitive Methodist household where she was raised. She told me that they never went to the theatre or an art gallery or a concert, and she never hit the arts at all until she went to Oxford when she occasionally went to concerts with friends. That was her first brush with the creative arts and she was modest about this . . . She said the same sort of thing in her speech. I was just getting my notes together to make mine and she suddenly said, "I hope you're not going to be funny. I find it a terrible waste of time and energy going to a dinner and listening to twelve familiar anecdotes about an Englishman, a Scotsman and an Irishman or something. It's really a waste of an evening. I like to learn something from after-dinner speeches, not just listen to amiable waffle." Fortunately, it was nearly the end of the evening, and I was feeling quite relaxed by then.'

Some would have crumpled under this formidable woman's exhortation. Hugh performed with his usual adept professionalism. He had never had lessons in public speaking – perhaps his projection would have been better if he had – but he knew just when to change the tone or rhythm of what he was saying, or bring in an unexpected or amusing comment

41

to wake people up.' I was speaking about two or three times a week during the Academy time. There are certain people you see in an audience, you can spot them clasping a handbag on their knees, with an expression of "Now show me" on their faces, and you worked on that lady. You were determined to get her attention and interest. It's funny how they stand out in an audience. It's as if they've been lit by an internal glow of potential disapproval, and I used to notice that.'

On the occasion when Thatcher made her daunting remarks just as Hugh was about to begin his speech, nobody seems to remember whether she laughed at it or not, but it is unlikely that Casson trotted out the type of Englishman, Welshman joke she so detested. Such banalities were not his style either. He obviously had a soft spot for his Conservative Prime Minister too, despite his dislike of her politics. But then she was, some think, an attractive woman, a breed to which he invariably responded with enthusiasm. Norman Rosenthal, who became Exhibitions Secretary during Hugh's time, believed Thatcher was supportive of the Academy because she knew it was not a drain on the public purse.

Mrs Thatcher may have been sober enough to make Hugh Casson quail, but much innocent merriment has been derived from her husband Denis's reputed penchant for 'a good snort'. Here is a letter from the 'Dear Bill' column in *Private Eye*, actually composed by Wells and Ingrams but purporting to be from the Prime Minister's husband Denis Thatcher to his old golfing and drinking companion Bill Deedes, editor of the *Daily Telegraph*. In real life, of course, Denis . . . But stop. This way lies libel. Read for yourself and remember that any resemblance between fact and fiction is entirely coincidental.

10 Downing Street
Whitehall
21 December 1979

Dear Bill,

Oh God! I expect you saw that I made page two of the *Telegraph*. Not exactly calculated to ease my lot with the Boss over Yule. Talk about shits of hell: Fleet Street takes the biscuit. God knows I'm let off the leash seldom enough as it is, sitting in Downing Street all day long being told to lift my feet up every time little Cosgrove comes by with the hoover, and now this comes up.

What happened, Bill, was as follows: as you probably know, I've been toddling along to the Savoy for donkeys' years for some little do that Squiffy gets together in aid of Mentally Handicapped Referees or something of that nature, and I've never thought a thing about it. Quite a decent set of chaps, a few snorts, odd familiar face, all very agreeable. This year, it so happened, thanks to M's elevated status, one of the organisers who I think runs a garden centre just outside Maidstone said would I mind getting up on my hind legs and saying a word or two after the loyal toast. Anything on a sporting theme, absolutely off the record, press wallahs excluded and so on and so forth. I should have seen his form a mile off: a real greaser of the old school and HMG to boot.

Anyway the time trickled by, and come the great day

43

mind still a perfect blank. Boris gave me quite an amusing story about a Chinaman which wasn't really suitable, but as luck would have it as I ran into Hector Bellville in the bar as both of us had arrived rather early, and he was frightfully steamed up about the Olympics. Wasn't it a bit rich for the Russians to be practising all their general ghastliness and at the same time telling us that it's *verboten* for the All Black And Tans or whatever they're called – I can never remember which are ours and which are the Kiwis' – to go out to South Africa and kick the ball about with Brother Boer.

By about seven when the others arrived I felt pretty strongly on this issue and after a dozen or so glasses of plonk accompanying whatever it was we were given to toy with over dinner, I was raring to go. Honestly, Bill, I really believed I was on home ground. And judging by the ovation I got from the comrades and the odd bread roll flying through the air I formed the impression I'd gone down rather well. Some silly bugger wrapped himself up in the tablecloth afterwards, occasioning a certain *froideur* from the Toastmaster, but otherwise the horseplay was very mild and a good time was had by all – or so I thought.

Imagine my feelings when I was having one for the road in a little broom cupboard with Hercot and Co afterwards, when the garden centre fellow came creeping up, laid a hand around my shoulders and said he'd been so bowled over by my harangue that he'd taken the liberty of ringing up a friend of his on *The Times*, and that the chap had been absolutely cock-a-hoop, high time somebody spoke up, my views would reach a wider audience etc.

The memory of breakfast next morning is still too painful to be raked over in full: suffice it to say that the decibel counter shot right off the dial. Did I realise that Africa was an unexploded bomb and that I was jumping up and down on it in hobnailed boots, or words to that effect. I said nothing, and at the first lull in the firing put down smoke and retired upstairs to do my devotions. Eric was very decent. He came up after me looking very shaken and said would I like to spend a few days with him and his mother.

. . . If I don't see you before, the merriest of Christmasses to you and yours, and don't do anything I wouldn't do.

Yours,

DENIS

John Wells and Richard Ingrams

Talking of speaking under the influence, I heard the crime-writer H. R. F. Keating once addressing a particularly intimidating Inner Temple dinner and opening his remarks by saying, 'I have been discussing with one of the country's most learned and distinguished judges just how much alcohol it is proper to consume before speaking on occasions such as this. And I'm bound to have to tell you that on this occasion I think I've got it wrong.' He hadn't, of course. He had imbibed to perfection and spoke accordingly. He also got a laugh for his self-deprecating beginning.

There is a school of thought that says that before embarking on after-dinner stories one should drink nothing at
all. The great cricketer Denis Compton, who was known to
take a drink on a cold day, once told me how he was invited
to speak after a dinner at the Royal and Ancient at St
Andrews. The R and A is to golf what the Vatican is to
Roman Catholicism and Denis was apprehensive and anxious to steady his nerves with a sharpener. 'No, no,' said the
President, the Rt Hon. Willie Whitelaw, who was also keen
on the occasional dram, 'You mustn't have anything to
drink before your speech.' Denis was as good as gold, told
his stories with aplomb, and afterwards was taken off by
Whitelaw to the President's room where they drank single
malts into the small hours.

I remembered this advice when I found myself speaking
at the annual banquet of the Royal Warrant Holders' Association. This was a terrifying white tie and tails affair in the
ballroom at Grosvenor House in London. I was billed to
appear after the legendary Welsh fly-half, Cliff Morgan, and
the Royal Kiltmaker, Douglas Kinloch Anderson, so I felt as
if I was the punch-line in one of those ghastly jokes about
Welshmen, Scotchmen and Englishmen. The wines on this
occasion were sumptuous but I thought of Denis and drank
nothing but water. Meanwhile glass after glass lined up on
the table in front of me. Vintage champagne, chateau-
bottled Chablis, red burgundy, Sauternes . . . I drank never
a drop, promising myself that when I finished my speech and
sat down I would quaff the lot. I made my speech, quivering
with sober-sided fright, sat down and reached out for the
first glass. As I did I heard the stentorian sound of our toastmaster bawling out 'My Lords, ladies and gentlemen, pray
be upstanding for your president and your guests of honour'
. . .' And before I could touch a drop of the assorted nectars
I was marched out of the hall to the strains of Handel and
the rhythmic clapping of the multitude.

The Royal Warrant Holders have, of course, been giving

46

extravagant banquets for the best part of two hundred years and, before I was interrupted by this prolonged drinks interval, I was dealing with a world several hundreds of years before Compton or even Wodehouse. So let us return, ladies and gentlemen, to an earlier time. In the early nineteenth century the banquets of the King's Tradesmen were absolutely stuffed with food, drink and words. The words were toasts rather than stories but they were absolutely part and parcel of the dining of the day. Here is an account of the epic of 1836, when William IV was on the throne, fifty or so years after Townshend's champagne speech to Parliament.

On His Majesty's birthday

On yesterday evening the tradesmen of the King dined together at the Thatched House tavern, St James's-street, in pursuance of their annual custom of celebrating his Majesty's birthday by a festive meeting. Though the anniversary dinners of several of the incorporated trading societies of the city of London take place on the 29th of May, yet more than fifty of the most respectable of his Majesty's tradesmen sat down on this occasion to a dinner provided in a very liberal and excellent style, and the feelings that pervaded the assemblage that characterised the meeting were

illustrative, in a highly gratifying degree, of the most enthusiastic and grateful attachment to our most gracious
monarch. The duties of chairman were admirably and satis-
factorily discharged by Mr Barwise, who presided on the
occasion, and the exertions of Messrs Robinson, Walker,
Novello, and Master Turner, greatly enhanced the hilarity of
the evening.

The discussion of the viands having concluded, and the
cloth having been drawn, *non nobis domine* was sung by the
professional gentlemen who attended.

The CHAIRMAN called for a bumper, and said that the state
of his Majesty's health, which had prevented his attendance
at Court that day, was a subject of deep concern to the
country, but in no portion of the community was the cause
of his Majesty's absence more deeply regretted than in that
room. [Cheers.] He hoped that his Majesty would speedily
be restored to the enjoyment of health, and that the country
would for many years to come be destined to enjoy the happiness of his paternal sway. [Cheers.] With feelings of the
deepest, most dutiful, most grateful, and loyal attachment
to his Majesty – feelings which he was sure would nowhere
find a more ardent or enthusiastic response than in the
breasts of those whom he saw around him – [loud cheers] –
he begged to propose 'The health of his Majesty the King'.
[Great cheering.]

The toast was drunk with nine times nine and the utmost
enthusiasm.

Song – 'God save the King', by Messrs Robinson, Walker,
&c.

The CHAIRMAN again rose and called for a brimming
bumper. He had great pleasure in stating that the health of
the Queen was greatly improved, and that her Majesty was
now perfectly convalescent. [Loud cheering.] It must have
been a subject of deep regret to the ladies of England that
her Majesty – the illustrious ornament of her sex, and distinguished no less by her station than by her virtues – was

prevented by circumstances which the nation regretted from presiding at her Court that day. It was, however, a matter of congratulation to learn that her Majesty's health was rapidly improving, and he begged to propose 'The health of her Majesty the Queen'. [Loud cheering.]

Drunk with enthusiasm.

Song – 'Here's a health to the King and the Queen'.

The CHAIRMAN next said that, though the Princess Victoria was politically in the same station that she held before, yet she was arrived at that age in which she was capable, should circumstances render it necessary, to undertake the high duties of governing this great country. He hoped that that necessity would be far distant, and that their gracious King would still live many years; but it was gratifying to know that, however remote the event that should call her to the Throne, they possessed a Princess who lived in the hearts of the people of England. [Cheers.] He begged to propose 'the Princess Victoria and the rest of the Royal Family'. [Drunk with loud applause.]

Song – 'Come o'er the brook'.

The CHAIRMAN next proposed the health of those services which had contributed so greatly to the glory of England, 'The Army and Navy'. [Great enthusiasm.]

Song – 'Rule Britannia'.

The CHAIRMAN said that the next toast was one which it had always on similar occasions been customary to drink. He would not say more, but propose 'His Majesty's Ministers'. [This toast was drunk in solemn silence.]

Song – 'Wapping Old Stairs'.

The CHAIRMAN again rose, and said that there was nothing more identified with the stability of the Throne than the prosperity of the Church – that Church which conferred blessings of the highest kind upon the country. He was about to name one than whom no one felt a more ardent interest for that Church, 'The Archbishop of Canterbury and the Established Church'. [This toast was drunk with the most rapturous enthusiasm and all the honours.]

Song – 'See the chariot', &c.

The CHAIRMAN said that the national glory had been promoted and the character of England illustrated by the heroic deeds of her great commanders both by land and by sea. She had had her Nelsons, her Abercrombies, and her Marlboroughs, but she never yet possessed a chief the record of whose proud achievements would form a nobler page in her history than that of the distinguished individual whose health he was about to propose – 'The Duke of Wellington'. [Great and continued cheering.]

The CHAIRMAN next proposed 'Sir Robert Peel and the prosperity of the manufacturing interest'. The announcement of this toast was received with the most ardent gratification, and it was drunk with nine times nine, and one cheer more.

Song – 'A sweet little cherub sits smiling aloft'.

The CHAIRMAN said that, as the assembly consisted of the citizens of Westminster, he would propose the health of one distinguished as a soldier and a statesman, and one by none more highly valued than those present, 'Sir George Murray'. [Great and continued acclamation hailed the announcement of this toast, and it is almost superfluous to say that it was drunk with the greatest possible enthusiasm.]

Song – 'In the valley near the mill'.

Amongst the several other toasts subsequently drunk in the course of the evening were the following: – 'The Lord Chamberlain'; 'The Lord Steward of the King's Household'; 'The Marquis of Chandos and the Agricultural Interest'; 'The Commercial and Trading Interests of the country'; 'Sir Thomas Mash', &c.

The company separated at a late hour, looking forward to the enjoyment of many anniversary returns of the joyous occasion.

The King's Tradesmen

It is hard to believe, after all this evidence to the contrary, that an entire post-prandial occasion could be concocted out of a sort of communal refusal to tell stories or make speeches. But there is a famous example of such entertaining speechlessness. It happened after the dinner to celebrate the sixtieth birthday of Hilaire Belloc in 1930, and here is his friend G. K. Chesterton's account of it.

Speechlessness

One of the most amusing events of my life occurred when I took the chair for a private celebration of Belloc's sixtieth birthday. There were about forty people assembled; nearly all of them were what is called important in the public sense, and the rest were even more important in the private sense, as being his nearest intimates and connections. To me it was that curious experience, something between the Day of Judgment and a dream, in which men of many groups known to me at many times all appeared together as a sort of resurrection. Anybody will understand that feeling who has had, as most people have had, the experience of some total stranger stopping him in the street and saying, 'And how are the old set?' On such occasions I become acutely conscious of having belonged to a large number of old sets. Most of the people I knew well enough; but some of the younger I had known quite lately and others long ago; and they included, as do all such gatherings, those whom I had intended to enquire about, and never carried out my intention. Anyhow, they were of all sorts except the stupid sort; and the renewed comradeship stirred in me the memory of a hundred contro-versies. There was my old friend Bentley, who dated from my first days at school; and Eccles, who reminded me of the ear-liest political rows of the Pro-Boers; and Jack Squire (now Sir John) who first floated into my circle in the days of the *Eye-Witness* and my brother's campaign against corruption; and Duff Cooper, a rising young politician I had met but a month or so before, and A. P. Herbert of somewhat similar age; and the brilliant journalist I had long known as *Beach-comber*, and only recently known as Morton. It was to be, and was, a very jolly evening; there were to be no speeches. It was specially impressed upon me that there were to be no speeches. Only I, as presiding, was to be permitted to say a few words in presenting Belloc with a golden goblet mod-elled on certain phrases in his heroic poem in praise of wine, which ends by asking that such a golden cup should be the stirrup-cup of his farewell to friends:

And sacramental raise me the divine
Strong brother in God and last companion, wine.

I merely said a few words to the effect that such a ceremony might have been as fitting thousands of years ago, at the festival of a great Greek poet; and that I was confident that Belloc's sonnets and strong verse would remain like the cups and the carved epics of the Greeks. He acknowledged it briefly, with a sad good humour, saying he found that, by the age of sixty, he did not care very much whether his verse remained or not. 'But I am told,' he added with suddenly reviving emphasis, 'I am told that you begin to care again frightfully when you are seventy. In which case, I hope I shall die at sixty-nine.' And then we settled down to the feast of old friends, which was to be so happy because there were no speeches.

Towards the end of the dinner somebody whispered to me that it would perhaps be better if a word were said in acknowledgment of the efforts of somebody whose name I forget, who was supposed to have arranged the affair. I therefore briefly thanked him; and he still more briefly thanked me, but added that it was quite a mistake, because the real author of the scheme was Johnnie Morton, otherwise *Beachcomber*, who sat immediately on his right. Morton rose solemnly to acknowledge the abruptly transferred applause; glanced to his own right, and warmly thanked who-ever happened to be sitting there (I think it was Squire) for having inspired him with this grand conception of a banquet for Belloc. Squire arose, and with many courteous gestures, explained that the gentleman on his own right, Mr A. P. Herbert, had been the true and deep and ultimate inspiration of this great idea; and that it was only fitting that the secret of his initiative should be now revealed. By this time, the logic of the jest was in full gallop and could not be restrained; even if I had wished to restrain it. A. P. Herbert rose to the occasion with superb presence of mind, and gave the series quite a new and original turn. He is an excellent speaker; and, as we all know, an admirable author; but I never knew before that he is an admirable actor. For some reason best known to himself, he chose to pretend to be the oratorical official of some sort of Workmen's Benevolent Society, like the Oddfellows or the Foresters. He did not need to tell us that he was taking this part; in the tone of his voice, he told it in the first few words. I shall never forget the exactitude of the accent with which he said, 'I'm sure, friends, we're all very pleased to see ex-Druid Chesterton among us this evening.' But he also gave his speech a definite logical direction. He said it was not to 'im, but to our old and faithful friend Duff Cooper that this pleasant evening was really due. Duff Cooper, sitting next to him, then rose and in resolute and ringing tones delivered an imitation of a Liberal platform speech, full of invocations of his great leader Lloyd George. He explained, however, that Mr E. C. Bentley on his right, and not himself, had arranged this trib-ute to that pillar of political Liberalism, Mr Belloc. Bentley gave one glance to his own right, and rose with exactly that supercilious gravity that I had seen forty years ago in the debating-clubs of our boyhood; the memory of his balanced eye-glasses and bland solemnity came back to me across my life with such intensity as stirs the tears that are born of time.

He said, with his precise enunciation, that he had himself followed through life one simple and sufficient rule. In all problems that arose, he had been content to consult exclusively the opinion of Professor Eccles. In every detail of daily life, in his choice of a wife, of a profession, of a house, of a dinner, he had done no more than carry out whatever Professor Eccles might direct. On the present occasion, any appearance he might have had of arranging the Belloc banquet was in fact a mask for Professor Eccles' influence. Professor Eccles responded in a similar but even more restrained fashion, merely saying that he had been mistaken for the man next to him, the real founder of the feast; and so by fatal and unfaltering steps, the whole process went round the whole table; till every single human being there had made a speech. It is the only dinner I have ever attended, at which it was literally true that every diner made an after-dinner speech. And that was the very happy ending of that very happy dinner, at which there were to be no speeches.

G. K. Chesterton

This sounds like an immensely stylish and entertaining non-story but sometimes – and we've all been there – the failure of the after-dinner speakers is abject. One of the endearing characteristics of the British is that when this happens we hardly ever admit it. 'My dear fellow, splendid speech,' we say when we all know that the speaker has bored for Britain. 'Frightfully funny story,' we chuckle admiringly after the said story has fallen like a lead balloon on an innocent furry animal. I am, however, particularly fond of one example of magisterial rebuke when the after-dinner entertainment fell conspicuously short of requirement. This was from Sir Pelham Warner, otherwise known as 'Plum'.

'Plum' Warner, grandfather, improbably, of the brilliant feminist writer Marina, was a peppery stalwart of the Marylebone Cricket Club, G. O. 'Gubby' Allen, of whom he tells the tale, was later to become almost as much of a pillar of the club but at this stage in his life was the recently returned captain of an MCC cricket tour to Australia. At this celebratory dinner Allen was clearly expected to give an entertaining warts-and-all account of his adventures down under, but er . . . well . . . here's Plum's verdict on an after-dinner speech which turned out to be the oratorical equivalent of a golden duck. Out first ball.

Just not cricket

Later, on July 15, during Gentlemen v. Players there was a dinner at the Savoy, at which Colonel Astor presided. The Duke of Gloucester was present, and read a message which the King was graciously pleased to send. It was a great event in the history of the Club, but the speeches were not worthy of the occasion, and a frightful faux pas was committed when the names of Lord Harris and of W. G. were not even mentioned – and they the only two men to whom permanent memorials have been erected at Lord's. To Allen, who had done so well in Australia, earning praise for his captaincy on the field and for his tact and general attitude off it, putting the cricketing relations between the two countries back on its old happy footing, was entrusted the reply to the toast of 'Cricket', which had been proposed by Sir Stanley Jackson. We were all looking forward to hearing from him something of the inside story of his interesting and exciting tour, but he confined his remarks almost entirely to the preparation of wickets and never said a word about the tour, or about Bradman, his opposite number, whose wonderful batting had won the rubber, for England had been victorious in the first two Test Matches, or about the great hospitality of the most hospitable people in the world.

Sir Pelham Warner

Ouch! One wouldn't want to have been Gubby Allen. Ladies and gentlemen, I have digressed. Digression is part and parcel of after-dinnery storytelling and speechifying. One starts with a clear purpose and a certain aim but one is deflected down constant anecdotal culs-de-sac and incidental asides, always mindful of the fact that it is the travelling and not the arriving which makes the journey worthwhile.

We were, if you recall, at the Royal Tradesmen's dinner of 1836 when I was led into yet another bibulous side-road containing G. K. Chesterton and Sir Pelham Warner. I propose now, with your permission, to reverse onto the main highway and return to the early-ish years of the nineteenth century. It was my former Medieval History tutor, Maurice Keen, who suggested the next odd fragment. He was not encouraging on the subject of oratory after dinner in medieval England. 'Not quite the stuff Matthew Parris went in for reporting,' he says.

However, he did come up with this piece of Gothick verse from the Revd R. H. Barham's *Ingoldsby Legends.* It's not exactly side-splitting but it has genuine curiosity value. 'A good pseudo-medieval speech', says Dr Keen. It is quintessentially Victorian.

From 'The Lay of St Cuthbert'

Hark! – as sure as fate
The clock's striking Eight!
(An hour which our ancestors called 'getting late'.)
When Nick, who by this time was rather elate,
Rose up and addressed them.
    ' 'Tis full time,' he said,
'For all elderly Devils to be in their bed;
For my own part I mean to be jogging, because
I don't find myself now quite so young as I was;
But, Gentlemen, ere I depart from my post,
I must call on you all for one bumper – the toast
Which I have to propose is, – OUR EXCELLENT HOST!
– Many thanks for his kind hospitality – may
We also be able,
    To see at *our* table
Himself, and enjoy, in a family way,
His good company *down stairs* at no distant day!
    You'd
I'm sure, think me rude
If I did not include
In the toast my young friend there, the curly-wig'd Heir.
He's in very good hands, for you're all well aware
That St Cuthbert has taken him under his care;
Though I must not say 'bless', –
    – Why you'll easily guess, –
May our curly-wig'd Friend's shadow never be less!'
Nick took off his heel-taps – bow'd – smiled – with an air
Most graciously grim, – and vacated the chair. –
    Of course the *élite*

Rose at once on their feet,
And followed their leader, and beat a retreat;
When a sky-larking Imp took the President's seat,
And, requesting that each would replenish his cup,
Said, 'Where we have dined, my boys, there let us sup!' –
– It was three in the morning before they broke up!!!

Revd R. H. Barham

After-dinner speaking and storytelling really came into their own during the nineteenth century. Indeed I submit, ladies and gentlemen, that, provided you had an hour or two to spare, this was the moment at which after-dinner entertainment was at its best. Brevity was not yet a virtue. Lincoln's Gettysburg address, for example, was dismissed at the time because it was thought insultingly short: 237 words heavily edited after dinner the night before! Today, in our fast-food, sound-bite age, many people have produced stories and bons mots on the merits of not banging on too long. Isaiah Berlin, *penseur*, savant, legendary Fellow of All Souls, once quoted a Lord Chief Justice: 'On occasions of this kind there are two speeches which I can make; one is short and one is long. The short one is "Thank you", the long one is "Thank you very much". Now that I have acquainted you with the content of both speeches I see no reason for making either.' Or, as Henry VIII said to his wives, 'I won't keep you long' . . .

But the Victorians, if at times distinctly florid, delivered their speeches with style. Here is one of the most celebrated of Victorians, Charles Dickens, addressing an audience of two hundred at Delmonico's, New York, where his hosts were the New York Press. Dickens's biographer John Forster tells us that Dickens attended with difficulty and spoke with pain but he so valued the speech that he attached it to every subsequent edition of his novel *Martin Chuzzlewit* and his *American Notes*. It is not a funny story, rather an apology to the American people for intemperate remarks made twenty-five years earlier on his first visit. 'They certainly are not a humorous people', was his verdict in 1843, 'and their temperament always impressed me as being of a dull and gloomy character.' His public repentance twenty-five years later makes an interesting counterpoint to the more familiar, jovial Dickens writing in *The Pickwick Papers*.

PS America

So much of my voice has lately been heard in the land, that I might have been contented with troubling you no further from my present standing-point, were it not a duty with which I henceforth charge myself, not only here but on every suitable occasion, whatsoever and wheresoever, to express my high and grateful sense of my second reception in America, and to bear my honest testimony to the national generosity and magnanimity. Also, to declare how astounded I have been by the amazing changes I have seen around me on every side, – changes moral, changes physical, changes in the amount of land subdued and peopled, changes in the rise of vast new cities, changes in the growth of older cities almost out of recognition, changes in the graces and amenities of life, changes in the Press, without whose advancement no advancement can take place anywhere. Nor am I, believe me, so arrogant as to suppose that in five and twenty years there have been no changes in me, and that I had nothing to learn and no extreme impressions to correct when I was here first. And this brings me to a point on which I have, ever since I landed in the United States last November, observed a strict silence, though sometimes tempted to break it, but in reference to which I will, with your good leave, take you into my confidence now. Even the Press, being human, may be sometimes mistaken or misinformed, and I rather think that I have in one or two rare instances observed its information to be not strictly accurate with reference to myself. Indeed, I have, now and again, been more surprised by printed news that I have read of myself, than by any printed news that I have ever read in my present state of existence. Thus, the vigour and perseverance with which I have for some months past been collecting materials for, and hammering away at, a new book on America has much astonished me; seeing that all that time my declaration has been perfectly well known to my publishers on both sides of the Atlantic, that no consideration on earth would induce me to write one. But what I have intended, what I have resolved upon (and this is the confidence I seek to place in you) is, on my return to England, in my own person, in my own Journal, to bear, for the behoof of my countrymen, such testimony to the gigantic changes in this country as I have hinted at tonight. Also, to record that wherever I have been, in the smallest places equally with the largest, I have been received with unsurpassable politeness, delicacy, sweet temper, hospitality, consideration, and with unsurpassable respect for the privacy daily enforced upon me by the nature of my avocation here and the state of my health. This testimony, so long as I live, and so long as my descendants have any legal right in my books, I shall cause to be republished, as an appendix to every copy of those two books of mine in which I have referred to America. And this I will do and cause to be done, not in mere love and thankfulness, but because I regard it as an act of plain justice and honour.

Charles Dickens

Dickens was celebrated as a great speaker and storyteller, but what were oratorical virtues for the Victorians have become speaker's warts for the New Elizabethans. Just as we are no longer comfortable with a profusion of words, so we can no longer cope with such enormous quantities of food and drink. Dickens's novels, however, stand the test of time. His fictional account of what went on after a nineteenth-century dinner is as fresh and vivid and funny as it would have seemed a hundred and fifty years ago.

Here, ladies and gentlemen, is Dickens describing the dinner after the cricket match between Dingley Dell and All Muggleton. Like so much of English life, village cricket has changed in its outward manifestations and yet it has not changed in its inner self. The after-match celebrations are Pickwickian (one might almost say Falstaffian) and there are elements which are utterly, well, Dickensian. On the other hand, anyone who has ever been to a village cricket club dinner will feel instantly at home.

Dingley Dell v. All Muggletonians

'We are about to partake of a plain dinner at the Blue Lion, sir; we hope you and your friends will join us.'

'Of course,' said Mr Wardle, 'among our friends we include Mr ——;' and he looked towards the stranger.

'Jingle,' said that versatile gentleman, taking the hint at once. 'Jingle – Alfred Jingle, Esq., of No Hall, Nowhere.'

'I shall be very happy, I am sure,' said Mr Pickwick.

'So shall I,' said Mr Alfred Jingle, drawing one arm through Mr Pickwick's, and another through Mr Wardle's, as he whispered confidentially in the ear of the former gentleman: –

'Devilish good dinner – cold, but capital – peeped into the room this morning – fowls and pies, and all that sort of thing – pleasant fellows these – well behaved, too – very.'

There being no further preliminaries to arrange, the

company straggled into the town in little knots of twos and threes; and within a quarter of an hour were all seated in the great room of the Blue Lion Inn, Muggleton – Mr Dumkins acting as chairman, and Mr Luffey officiating as vice.

There was a vast deal of talking and rattling of knives and forks, and plates: a great running about of three ponderous-headed waiters, and a rapid disappearance of the substantial viands on the table; to each and every of which item of confusion, the facetious Mr Jingle lent the aid of half-a-dozen ordinary men at least. When everybody had eaten as much as

possible, the cloth was removed, bottles, glasses, and dessert were placed on the table; and the waiters withdrew to 'clear away', or in other words, to appropriate to their own private use and emolument, whatever remnants of the eatables and drinkables they could contrive to lay their hands on.

Amidst the general hum of mirth and conversation that ensued, there was a little man with a puffy Say-nothing-to-me-,-or-I'll-contradict-you sort of countenance, who remained very quiet; occasionally looking round him when the conversation slackened, as if he contemplated putting in something very weighty; and now and then bursting into a short cough of inexpressible grandeur. At length, during a moment of comparative silence, the little man called out in a very loud, solemn voice —

'Mr Luffey!'

Everybody was hushed into a profound stillness as the individual addressed, replied —

'Sir?'

'I wish to address a few words to you, sir, if you will entreat the gentlemen to fill their glasses.'

Mr Jingle uttered a patronising 'hear, hear,' which was responded to by the remainder of the company: and the glasses having been filled the Vice-President assumed an air of wisdom in a state of profound attention, and said —

'Mr Staple.'

'Sir,' said the little man, rising, 'I wish to address what I have to say to *you* and not to our worthy chairman, because our worthy chairman is in some measure — I may say in a great degree — the subject of what I have to say, or I may say to —'

'State,' suggested Mr Jingle.

— 'Yes, to state,' said the little man. 'I thank my honourable friend, if he will allow me to call him so — (four "hears," and one certainly from Mr Jingle) — for the suggestion. Sir, I am a Deller — a Dingley Deller (cheers). I cannot lay claim to the honour of forming an item in the population of Muggleton; nor, sir, I will frankly admit, do I covet that honour: and I will tell you why, sir – (hear); to Muggleton I will readily concede all those honours and distinctions to which it can fairly lay claim – they are too numerous and too well known to require aid or recapitulation from me. But, sir, while we remember that Muggleton has given birth to a Dumkins and a Podder, let us never forget that Dingley Dell can boast a Luffey and a Struggles. (Vociferous cheering.) Let me not be considered as wishing to detract from the merits of the former gentlemen. Sir, I envy them the luxury of their own feelings on this occasion. (Cheers.) Every gentleman who hears me, is probably acquainted with the reply made by an individual, who – to use an ordinary figure of speech – "hung out" in a tub, to the emperor Alexander: – "If I were not Diogenes," said he, "I would be Alexander." I can well imagine these gentlemen to say, "If I were not Dumkins I would be Luffey; if I were not Podder I would be Struggles." (Enthusiasm.) But, gentlemen of Muggleton, is it in cricket alone that your fellow-townsmen stand pre-eminent? Have you never heard of Dumkins and determination? Have you never been taught to associate Podder with property? (Great applause.) Have you never, when struggling for your rights, your liberties, and your privileges, been reduced, if only for an instant, to misgiving and despair? And when you have been thus depressed, has not the name of Dumkins laid afresh within your breast the fire which had just gone out; and has not a word from that man, lighted it again as brightly as if it had never expired? (Great cheering.) Gentlemen, I beg to surround with a rich halo of enthusiastic cheering the united names of "Dumkins and Podder." '

Here the little man ceased, and here the company commenced a raising of voices, and thumping of tables, which lasted with little intermission during the remainder of the evening. Other toasts were drunk. Mr Luffey and Mr Struggles, Mr Pickwick and Mr Jingle, were, each in his turn, the subject of unqualified eulogium; and each in due course returned thanks for the honour.

Enthusiastic as we are in the noble cause to which we have devoted ourselves, we should have felt a sensation of pride which we cannot express, and a consciousness of having done something to merit immortality of which we are now deprived, could we have laid the faintest outline of these addresses before our ardent readers. Mr Snodgrass, as usual, took a great mass of notes, which would no doubt have afforded most useful and valuable information, had not the burning eloquence of the words or the feverish influence of the wine made that gentleman's hand so extremely unsteady, as to render his writing nearly unintelligible, and his style wholly so. By dint of patient investigation, we have been enabled to trace some characters bearing a faint resemblance to the names of the speakers; and we can also discern an entry of a song (supposed to have been sung by Mr Jingle), in which the words 'bowl', 'sparkling', 'ruby', 'bright', and 'wine' are frequently repeated at short intervals. We fancy too, that we can discern at the very end of the notes, some indistinct reference to 'broiled bones'; and then the words 'cold' 'without' occur: but as any hypothesis we could found upon them must necessarily rest upon mere conjecture, we are not disposed to indulge in any of the speculations to which they may give rise.

We will therefore return to Mr Tupman; merely adding that within some few minutes before twelve o'clock that night, the convocation of worthies of Dingley Dell and Muggleton were heard to sing, with great feeling and emphasis, the beautiful and pathetic national air of

We won't go home 'till morning,
We won't go home 'till morning,
We won't go home 'till morning,
'Till daylight doth appear.

An even more memorable cricket match than the one between Dingley Dell and All Muggleton was the one between
Mr Hodge's wandering team and the village of Fordenden in
A. G. Macdonell's *England, Their England*. That too led to
drinking and impromptu post-prandial speechifying. You
will recall, ladies and gentlemen, that after the match 'both
teams spent the evening at the Three Horseshoes and Mr
Harcourt made a speech in Italian about the glories of England and afterwards fell asleep in a corner, and Donald got
home to Royal Avenue at 1 o'clock in the morning, feeling
that he had not learnt very much about the English from his
experience of their national game.'

Perhaps it was an occasion like those described by
Richard Ingrams in his introduction to *The Best of Beach-
comber*. The inimitable J. B. Morton shared a flat with the
assistant editor of *The London Mercury*, the poet Edward
Shanks, and the two of them formed part of the group of
poets and writers who gathered round J. C. Squire, the editor of the same.

Ballades and Beachcomber

Both were regular attenders at the annual dinners at the
Cheshire Cheese given by Squire's cricket club, the Invalids,
which always ended in a sing-song. Morton sang 'En Passant
par la Lorraine' and Belloc's 'The Winged Horse'. Someone
else sang the doleful ditty 'I want to be buried in Rutland

if there's room'. The company included, in addition to Squire's 'set', G. K. Chesterton and Hilaire Belloc. Chester-ton, not a musical man, was sufficiently impressed by Mor-ton's performance to be able to reproduce in later years his rendition of the following song:

In my garden there are rowziz
Rowziz red and violets blew:
In my garden there is sunshine
In my garden there is yew! (*top note*)
(*Angry undertone*) Ya bloody worm.

Another man who came to these sing-songs was Chester-ton's old friend E. C. Bentley, author of *Trent's Last Case*. ... Bentley was responsible for reviving, when at Oxford, the old French verse form of the Ballade, which was taken up by Belloc and subsequently became a bit of a craze. The poem has a stringent rhyming scheme and demands a good deal of skill. In 1931 Squire edited a collection,* to which Belloc, Maurice Baring, he himself, Chesterton, Bentley and Morton all contributed. The most prolific ballade-writer was Hugh Mackintosh, also a devoted admirer of Squire and Belloc, and a close friend of Morton's. One ballade by Mackintosh, redolent of the period, went as follows:

BALLADE IN MEMORY
OF 'THE ANGEL', PETWORTH

We have sung songs at many times and places –
The easeful songs of laughter and of war:
In lusty tenors, baritones and basses
We've chanted ditties from our boundless store:
And yet it's vain attempting to ignore
This hard and bitter fact – it's no use blinking,
The truth will out (it shakes us to the core) –
We sing a great deal better when we're drinking.

* *101 Ballades*, Cobden Sanderson, 1931.

By tavern fires, ringed round with friendly faces,
Have we not heard the cries: 'Bravo! . . . Encore!'
And sung, so loudly that we've burst our braces,
Shanty and round – and still they've asked for more?
What verve, what golden notes, what vocal lore
Are ours, when seated in a tap room sinking
A pint or two! – yes (even from the floor)
We sing a great deal better when we're drinking.

But in the morning ('tis perhaps the traces,
The tuneful efforts, of the night before)
Our voices – say in church – might cause grimaces,
While at the Wigmore Hall we might not score
A quarter of our usual furore.
Come then at nightfall to 'The Angel', linking
Arm in affectionate arm, a happy four:
We sing a great deal better when we're drinking.

ENVOI

Prince, when you hear afar the ring and roar
Of voices singing and of tankards chinking,
Fear not, my friend, come in and shut the door!
We sing a great deal better when we're drinking.

69

This particular ballade was dedicated to Morton, Peter Belloc and Jim Allison, who, with Mackintosh, made up the 'happy four' referred to. It was at the Angel, Petworth, that Morton offered a quart of beer to anyone who could hit him on the nose with a ball on a string, used for knocking down skittles.

Richard Ingrams

Meanwhile – that is, at much the same time as Charles Dickens was telling the story of the cricket match dinner at Dingley Dell – on the other side of the Atlantic our American cousins were demonstrating once again that we are two countries divided by a common language. As Scott Fitzgerald observed of the rich, and L. P. Hartley of the past, the United States is a foreign country and they do things differently there.

Henry Grady's speech to the New England Society of New York, celebrating 'The New South' in the aftermath of the American Civil War, is widely held in the United States to be the after-dinner business, the *ne plus ultra*, the acme of *après*-dinner entertainment. It's stirring stuff – on the long side, perhaps, to modern English ears, but wonderfully orotund. Here is the first part of it.

The New South

Mr President and gentlemen: Let me express to you my appreciation of the kindness by which I am permitted to address you. I make this abrupt acknowledgment advisedly, for I feel that if, when I raise my provincial voice in this ancient and august presence, I could find courage for no more than the opening sentence, it would be well if, in that sentence, I had met in a rough sense my obligation as a guest, and had perished, so to speak, with courtesy on my lips and grace in my heart. [Laughter.] Permitted through your kindness to catch my second wind, let me say that I appreciate the significance of being the first Southerner to speak at this board, which bears the substance, if it surpasses the semblance, of original New England hospitality [applause], and honors a sentiment that in turn honors you, but in which my personality is lost, and the compliment to my people made plain. [Laughter.]

I bespeak the utmost stretch of your courtesy tonight. I am not troubled about those from whom I come. You

remember the man whose wife sent him to a neighbor with
a pitcher of milk, and who, tripping on the top step, fell,
with such casual interruptions as the landing afforded, into
the basement; and while picking himself up had the pleasure
of hearing his wife call out: 'John, did you break the
pitcher?'

'No, I didn't,' said John, 'but I be dinged if I don't!'
[Laughter.] So, while those who call to me from behind may
inspire me with energy if not with courage, I ask an indul-
gent hearing from you. I beg that you will bring your full
faith in American fairness and frankness of judgment upon
what I shall say. There was an old preacher once who told
some boys of the Bible lesson he was going to read in the
morning. The boys, finding the place, glued together the
connecting pages. [Laughter.] The next morning he read on
the bottom of one page: 'When Noah was one hundred and
twenty years old he took unto himself a wife, who was' –
then turning the page – 'one hundred and forty cubits long
[laughter], forty cubits wide, built of gopher-wood [laugh-
ter], and covered with pitch inside and out.' [Loud and
continued laughter.] He was naturally puzzled at this. He
read it again, verified it, and then said: 'My friends, this is
the first time I ever met this in the Bible, but I accept it as an
evidence of the assertion that we are fearfully and wonderfully made.' [Immense laughter.] If I could get you to hold
such faith tonight I could proceed cheerfully to the task I
otherwise approach with a sense of consecration.

Pardon me one word, Mr President, spoken for the sole purpose of getting into the volumes that go out annually freighted with the rich eloquence of your speakers – the fact that the Cavalier as well as the Puritan was on the continent in its early days, and that he was 'up and able to be about'. [Laughter.] I have read your books carefully and I find no mention of that fact, which seems to me an important one for preserving a sort of historical equilibrium if for nothing else.

Let me remind you that the Virginia Cavalier first challenged France on this continent – that Cavalier John Smith gave New England its very name, and was so pleased with the job that he has been handing his own name around ever since – and that while Miles Standish was cutting off men's ears for courting a girl without her parents' consent, and forbade men to kiss their wives on Sunday, the Cavalier was courting everything in sight, and that the Almighty had vouchsafed great increase to the Cavalier colonies, the huts in the wilderness being full as the nests in the woods.

But having incorporated the Cavalier as a fact in your charming little books I shall let him work out his own salvation, as he has always done with engaging gallantry, and we will hold no controversy as to his merits. Why should we? Neither Puritan nor Cavalier long survived as such. The virtues and traditions of both happily still live for the inspiration of their sons and the saving of the old fashion. [Applause.] But both Puritan and Cavalier were lost in the storm of the first Revolution; and the American citizen, supplanting both and stronger than either, took possession of the Republic bought by their common blood and fashioned to wisdom, and charged himself with teaching men government and establishing the voice of the people as the voice of God. [Applause.]

My friend Dr Talmage has told you that the typical American has yet to come. Let me tell you that he has already come. [Applause.] Great types like valuable plants are slow to flower and fruit. But from the union of these colonist Puritans and Cavaliers, from the straightening of their purposes and the crossing of their blood, slow perfecting through a century, came he who stands as the first typical American, the first who comprehended within himself all the strength and gentleness, all the majesty and grace of this Republic – Abraham Lincoln. [Loud and continued applause.] He was the sum of Puritan and Cavalier, for in his ardent nature were fused the virtues of both, and in the depths of his great soul the faults of both were lost. [Renewed applause.] He was greater than Puritan, greater than Cavalier, in that he was American [renewed applause] and that in his homely form were first gathered the vast and thrilling forces of his ideal government – charging it with such tremendous meaning and so elevating it above human suffering that martyrdom, though infamously aimed, came as a fitting crown to a life consecrated from the cradle to human liberty. [Loud and prolonged cheering.] Let us, each cherishing the traditions and honoring his fathers, build with reverent hands to the type of this simple but sublime life, in which all types are honored; and in our common glory as Americans there will be plenty and to spare for your forefathers and for mine. [Renewed cheering.]

In speaking to the toast with which you have honored me, I accept the term, 'The New South', as in no sense disparaging to the Old. Dear to me, sir, is the home of my childhood and the traditions of my people. I would not, if I could, dim the glory they won in peace and war, or by word or deed take aught from the splendor and grace of their civilization – never equaled and, perhaps, never to be equaled in its chivalric strength and grace. There is a New South, not through protest against the Old, but because of new conditions, new adjustments and, if you please, new ideas and aspirations. It is to this that I address myself, and to the consideration of which I hasten lest it become the Old South before I get to it. Age does not endow all things with strength and virtue, nor are all new things to be despised. The shoemaker who put over his door 'John Smith's shop. Founded in 1760,' was more than matched by his young rival across the street who hung out this sign: 'Bill Jones. Established 1886. No old stock kept in this shop.'

Dr Talmage has drawn for you, with a master's hand, the picture of your returning armies. He has told you how, in the pomp and circumstance of war, they came back to you, marching with proud and victorious tread, reading their glory in a nation's eyes! Will you bear with me while I tell you of another army that sought its home at the close of the late war – an army that marched home in defeat and not in victory – in pathos and not in splendor, but in glory that equaled yours, and to hearts as loving as ever welcomed heroes home. Let me picture to you the footsore Confederate soldier, as, buttoning up in his faded gray jacket the parole which was to bear testimony to his children of his fidelity and faith, he turned his face southward from Appomattox in April, 1865. Think of him as ragged, half-starved, heavy-hearted, enfeebled by want and wounds; having fought to exhaustion, he surrenders his gun, wrings the

hands of his comrades in silence, and lifting his tear-stained and pallid face for the last time to the graves that dot the old Virginia hills, pulls his gray cap over his brow and begins the slow and painful journey. What does he find – let me ask you, who went to your homes eager to find in the welcome you had justly earned, full payment for four years' sacrifice – what does he find when, having followed the battle-stained cross against overwhelming odds, dreading death not half so much as surrender, he reaches the home he left so prosper- ous and beautiful? He finds his house in ruins, his farm dev- astated, his slaves free, his stock killed, his barns empty, his trade destroyed, his money worthless; his social system, feu- dal in its magnificence, swept away; his people without law or legal status, his comrades slain, and the burdens of others heavy on his shoulders. Crushed by defeat, his very traditions are gone; without money, credit, employment, material or training; and, besides all this, confronted with the gravest problem that ever met human intelligence – the establishing of a status for the vast body of his liberated slaves.

Henry W. Grady

A speaker, a pro, and a match in his day for Charles Dickens himself, at least as an after-dinner orator if not as a novelist (though some Americans would disagree), was Mark Twain. It was Twain who said that there are 'three kinds of lies – lies, damned lies and statistics', and Twain who said that 'it is by the goodness of God that we have in our country three unspeakably precious things: freedom of speech, freedom of conscience and the prudence never to practice either.' In this, Twain was guilty of telling a statistic. He made exceed- ing free with speech, as we see from the following speech, made at a dinner given by the publishers of *The Atlantic Monthly* in Boston in 1877.

This is an occasion peculiarly meet for the digging up of pleasant reminiscences concerning literary folk; therefore I will drop lightly into history myself. Standing here on the shore of the Atlantic and contemplating certain of its largest literary billows, I am reminded of a thing which happened to me thirteen years ago, when I had just succeeded in stirring up a little Nevadian literary puddle myself, whose spume-flakes were beginning to blow thinly Californiaward. I started an inspection tramp through the southern mines of California. I was callow and conceited, and I resolved to try the virtue of my *nom de guerre*.

I very soon had an opportunity. I knocked at a miner's lonely log cabin in the foot-hills of the Sierras just at night-fall. It was snowing at the time. A jaded, melancholy man of fifty, barefooted, opened the door to me. When he heard my *nom de guerre* he looked more dejected than before. He let me in – pretty reluctantly, I thought – and after the customary bacon and beans, black coffee and hot whiskey, I took a pipe. This sorrowful man had not said three words up to this time. Now he spoke up and said, in the voice of one who is secretly suffering, 'You're the fourth – I'm going to move.' 'The fourth what?' said I. 'The fourth littery man that has been here in twenty-four hours – I'm going to move.' 'You don't tell me!' said I; 'who were the others?' 'Mr Longfellow, Mr Emerson, and Mr Oliver Wendell Holmes – confound the lot!'

You can easily believe I was interested. I supplicated – three hot whiskeys did the rest – and finally the melancholy miner began. Said he:

'They came here just at dark yesterday evening, and I let them in of course. Said they were going to the Yosemite. They were a rough lot, but that's nothing; everybody looks rough that travels afoot. Mr Emerson was a seedy little bit of a chap, red-headed. Mr Holmes was as fat as a balloon; he weighed as much as three hundred, and had double chins all the way down to his stomach. Mr Longfellow was built like a prize-fighter. His head was cropped and bristly, like as if he had a wig made of hair-brushes. His nose lay straight down his face, like a finger with the end joint tilted up. They had been drinking, I could see that. And what queer talk they used! Mr Holmes inspected this cabin, then he took me by the buttonhole, and says he:

' "Through the deep caves of thought
I hear a voice that sings,
Build thee more stately mansions,
O my soul!"

'Says I, "I can't afford it, Mr Holmes, and moreover I don't want to." Blamed if I liked it pretty well, either, coming from a stranger, that way. However, I started to get out my bacon and beans, when Mr Emerson came and looked on awhile, and then *he* takes me aside by the buttonhole and says:

' "Give me agates for my meat;
Give me cantharids to eat;
From air and ocean bring me foods,
From all zones and altitudes."

'Says I, "Mr Emerson, if you'll excuse me, this ain't no hotel." You see it sort of riled me – I warn't used to the ways of littery swells. But I went on a-sweating over my work, and next comes Mr Longfellow and buttonholes me, and interrupts me. Says he:

' "Honor be to Mudjekeewis!
You shall hear how Pau-Puk-Keewis—"

'But I broke in, and says I, "Beg your pardon, Mr Long-fellow, if you'll be so kind as to hold your yawp for about five minutes and let me get this grub ready, you'll do me proud." Well, sir, after they'd filled up I set out the jug. Mr Holmes looks at it, and then he fires up all of a sudden and yells:

    ' "Flash out a stream of blood-red wine!
    For I would drink to other days."

'By George, I was getting kind of worked up. I don't deny
it, I was getting kind of worked up. I turns to Mr Holmes,
and says I, "Looky here, my fat friend, I'm a-running this
shanty, and if the court knows herself, you'll take whiskey
straight or you'll go dry." Them's the very words I said to
him. Now I don't want to sass such famous littery people,
but you see they kind of forced me. There ain't nothing
onreasonable 'bout me; I don't mind a passel of guests
a-treadin' on my tail three or four times, but when it comes
to *standing* on it it's different, "and if the court knows

herself." I says, "you'll take whiskey straight or you'll go
dry." Well, between drinks they'd swell around the cabin and
strike attitudes and spout; and pretty soon they got out a
greasy old deck and went to playing euchre at ten cents a
corner – on trust. I began to notice some pretty suspicious
things. Mr Emerson dealt, looked at his hand, shook his
head, says:

' "I am the doubter and the doubt—"

and ca'mly bunched the hands and went to shuffling for a
new layout. Says he:

' "They reckon ill who leave me out;
They know not well the subtle ways I keep.
I pass and deal again!"

Hang'd if he didn't go ahead and do it, too! Oh, he was a
cool one! Well, in about a minute things were running
pretty tight, but all of a sudden I see by Mr Emerson's eye
he judged he had 'em. He had already corralled two tricks,
and each of the others one. So now he kind of lifts a little in
his chair and says:

' "I tire of globes and aces!—
Too long the game is played!"

– and down he fetched a right bower. Mr Longfellow smiles
as sweet as pie and says:

' "Thanks, thanks to thee, my worthy friend,
For the lesson thou hast taught,"

– and blamed if he didn't down with *another* right bower!
Emerson claps his hand on his bowie, Longfellow claps his
on his revolver, and I went under a bunk. There was going
to be trouble; but that monstrous Holmes rose up, wob-
bling his double chins, and says he, "Order, gentlemen; the
first man that draws, I'll lay down on him and smother
him!" All quiet on the Potomac, you bet!

'They were pretty how-come-you-so by now, and they begun to blow. Emerson says, "The nobbiest thing I ever wrote was 'Barbara Frietchie.'" Says Longfellow, "It don't begin with my 'Biglow Papers.'" Says Holmes, "My 'Thanatopsis' lays over 'em both." They mighty near ended in a fight. Then they wished they had some more company – and Mr Emerson pointed to me and says:

' "Is yonder squalid peasant all
   That this proud nursery could breed?"

He was a-whetting his bowie on his boot – so I let it pass. Well, sir, next they took it into their heads that they would like some music; so they made me stand up and sing "When Johnny Comes Marching Home" till I dropped – at thirteen minutes past four this morning. That's what I've been through, my friend. When I woke at seven, they were leaving, thank goodness, and Mr Longfellow had my only boots on, and his'n under his arm. Says I, "Hold on, there, Evangeline, what are you going to do with *them*?" He says, "Going to make tracks with 'em; because:

' "Lives of great men all remind us
   We can make our lives sublime;
And, departing, leave behind us
   Footprints on the sands of time."

As I said, Mr Twain, you are the fourth in twenty-four hours – and I'm going to move; I ain't suited to a littery atmosphere.'

I said to the miner, 'Why, my dear sir, *these* were not the gracious singers to whom we and the world pay loving reverence and homage; these were impostors.'

The miner investigated me with a calm eye for a while; then said he, 'Ah! impostors, were they? Are *you*?'

I did not pursue the subject, and since then I have not travelled on my *nom de guerre* enough to hurt. Such was the reminiscence I was moved to contribute, Mr Chairman. In my enthusiasm I may have exaggerated the details a little, but you will easily forgive me that fault, since I believe it is the first time I have ever deflected from perpendicular fact on an occasion like this.

Mark Twain

Dwelling on eminent Victorians, of whom Dickens and Twain were clearly two – even though Twain as an American might baulk at the idea – reminds me of Lytton Strachey's biographer, Michael Holroyd. Michael is a consummate after-dinner speaker and a veteran of countless literary repasts. He is also inclined to be forgetful. Sending me the passage that follows he was completely unable to remember when he had given it or where. He swears, however, that he delivered it after dinner. Had it been anyone else, I might have been inclined to be suspicious, but in Michael's case this is entirely characteristic. This is a man after all, ladies and gentlemen, who only knew that his regiment was about to invade Egypt during the Suez Crisis when he saw Pathé-news footage of his embarking comrades on a clandestine visit to his local cinema.

He is, as you can see, a man whose sense of time is precarious, so, since this speech begins with his Victorian grandfather, let us read it here. Ladies and gentlemen, Mr Michael Holroyd.

A prominent feature

When I was a child it was often difficult to get into the lavatory at home on account of my grandfather's shaving habits. He was not a skilful shaver. His chin and cheeks, as well as his neck and nose, were often dotted with blood-soaked tufts of cotton wool and crossed with thin red lines like

alleged Martian canals. Late in life, as an act of mercy, he had been given an electric razor. After some experimentation in the garage, he found this gadget easiest to use when he stood on the lavatory seat and plugged it into the dangling cord of the overhead light. In the darkness the whole operation lasted about three-quarters of an hour (for he sometimes mislaid part of his kit in the cistern). My aunt, my grandmother and myself would line up outside rattling the door handle and crying out in distress. But his hearing was not so good. Besides, he felt protected by the comfortable whirring of this electrical contraption. It soothed his nerves. Sometimes, it was true, he would shave one side of his face twice since there was no lather now to guide him. But over a week matters would even themselves out.

What impressed me about these arduous exercises was the obvious importance of appearing shaven in public – one could not really say clean-shaven with such a battlefield of a face. I think this must have impressed my father too. It was whispered that at the age of twenty he had sported a small moustache but quickly removed it after the rise of Hitler. When I questioned him about it he became embarrassed. This was not surprising as he had grown very very severe with anyone who, as he phrased it, 'had fungus on his face'. Statements syphoned through this mesh of hair always sounded like nonsense to him, and he was not above shouting abuse at bearded pundits when they appeared on television.

As the flower of this family tradition I grew up a beardless wonder. In fact I am not naturally a clean-shaven man. Like drinking whisky or eating olives, it is an acquired habit, and the stubble, fine and shadowy, is newly reaped each day. But I have found this achievement easier than my grandfather did. In the matter of chins there is nowhere further for Holroydian evolution to go. I am in its final statement. Some chins are determined, others, as P. G. Wodehouse noticed, give up the struggle about halfway down. My own chin belongs to neither of these categories. Though I never went to a university and have no academic degrees of any kind, my chin is a professorial chin, I maintain, which is to say it is an absent-minded chin. Naturally it does not appear like this to my family, but my family are not certain what I do for a living. I have no office and apparently spend much of my time at home reading. Possibly, it occurs to them, I am a spy. To those, however, who are sent to meet me at airports or railway stations on British Council lecture tours, this chin of mine is a most misleading feature. They take one look at it then walk straight past staring down the railway track or into the sky. It is inconceivable to them that the biographer of Lytton Strachey, Augustus John and Bernard Shaw, a famously hirsute trio, should have a naked chin. When I am obliged to present my passport as proof of my identity there is dismay, even a sense of being cheated. They wonder whether I am travelling incognito and wearing the equivalent of an opera singer's bald wig. To regain my authority I am developing a 'take-it-on-the-chin' ideology. My chin, after all, is the very symbol of my authorial individuality, a proud sign that I have not been submerged by my biographical subjects. It is as vital for the biographer as for the boxer not to have a suspect chin. As I write, my chin points to the very paper I write on – as sensitive as a dog's nose. One day, I suspect, it will give rise to a new school of literary theory. Meanwhile I regard it as part of my subtext and a clue to others that the biographer is not an actor made up to look like his subject, but a detective in deep disguise.

A beard, like a word-processor, is one of the things I positively do not have. I have a pen and a chin. Whenever I feel low I say to myself 'Chin Up!', grab my pen and throw off another volume or two.

Michael Holroyd

It is not customary to think of Sir Winston Churchill as an eminent Victorian and yet he was almost thirty years old by the time Queen Victoria died. As an after-dinner speaker he was often magisterial, sometimes, especially as the wartime Prime Minister, deadly serious. Yet for A. P. Herbert, no slouch himself on the humour front, he was the greatest humorist of them all.

Winston Churchill

At any moment, in any audience, whatever the emotional background, he can make them laugh when he wishes; and he can do so without any breach of taste or tact, and that is a pretty severe test. During the war, when he was making his dramatic speeches and the tension was just too much, out would come some charming, inimitable jest which made us all laugh – and feel better. He was a master in that art and it is a great pity that there was no Boswell to record him.

I remember one story of him before the war. A certain statesman had been making a rather woolly speech about the League of Nations and Foreign Affairs. Winston Churchill was asked what he thought of it and he said, 'Well, I thought it was very good. It must have been good because it contained, so far as I know, all the platitudes known to the human race, with the possible exception of "Prepare to meet thy God", and "Please adjust your dress before leaving".'

I remember many years ago, when I was not even a Member of Parliament and was very small fry indeed, being invited to lunch at Gen. Spears' house and there meeting Churchill and Sir Archibald Sinclair, and other great men. While they were drinking cocktails, somebody mentioned a politician who was very much in the limelight at that time. I thought that was my cue, so I said, 'Did you see that so-and-so's son has made his first speech?' and Winston Churchill said, 'Yes, I saw that, too, and I said to myself, "Is it not enough that we have this parent volcano continually erupting in our midst – and now we are to have these subsidiary craters spouting forth their filthy fumes?"'

A. P. Herbert

Here he is delivering a speech at the Corinthian Club in Dublin on 14 January 1904, in response to a fulsome introduction by Sir Charles Cameron. It is the third year of Edwardian England, and Churchill, still a young man, is at his most puckish and mercurial.

To the Corinthians

I was very anxious to get a little opportunity to prepare those impromptus to which Sir Charles Cameron has alluded, and I asked him at the beginning of the dinner if he would very kindly tell me what he was going to say. He told me he did not know what he was going to say, so I concluded he is among that style of orators who used to be familiar in the House of Commons, of whom it was said, 'Before they get up they do not know what they are going to say, while they are speaking they do not know what they are saying, and when they have sat down they do not know what they have said.'

I do not know whether Sir Charles is anxious to figure in that category. I do not know if he remembers now what he has been saying, but certain I am of this, that we remember it. I confess I think it no little test to expose an unwilling guest in compelling him to respond to a toast which has just been proposed by such a past master of after-dinner speaking as your President.

I regard it as a very great honour to have been allowed to come here tonight, and I think it very kind of you to have asked me during my short visit to Dublin. I have not a great many friends in Ireland, but I have a few inherited friends.

Some I have inherited from my grandfather, to whom Sir Charles Cameron has made a very complimentary allusion, and some I have inherited from my father. That is my estate in Ireland, and I can assure you I do not mean to sell it under the Land Act. I shall certainly not take twenty-five years' purchase for it.

I do not mean to neglect it; I mean to work it up, and certainly, so far as that estate is concerned, I shall not be an absentee landlord. Perhaps I have even been able upon this visit, sitting as I am next to Sir Charles Cameron, to add a little outlying plot to my inherited estate. Sir Charles Cameron has alluded to the fact that I have been a war cor-respondent, and he seems to think it a great advantage to a war correspondent to have been a soldier who had learned to ride a horse.

Well, the duties of a war correspondent are various and complicated. Sometimes he gives a general a dinner; some-times he tells a general what to do; sometimes he tells the public what a general ought to have done; and sometimes he tells the public what a general has done and sometimes he does not.

But whatever information a war correspondent sends home, he collects the information on the field, and whatever he sends home is published by the newspapers, a penny plain, a ha'penny coloured. Of course, it is quite true that this interesting profession is not without its danger. I think there were a great number of war correspondents in the South African War who lost their lives, who were wounded, who lost their limbs, or, for a more or less protracted period, lost their liberty. Some of them succeeded in recovering their liberty.

Three years ago I had the good fortune to come to Dublin to give a lecture on the subject of the South African War, and my experiences and adventures there. That great contest in which we were then engaged is now passed out of life into history, and a good deal of very mixed history has been written concerning it.

The war is over, but the difficulties in that country continue. I trust most earnestly that just because the war is over, the attention of the British and Irish people will not be altogether diverted from South Africa, because I am convinced that when we in these islands lose interest in what is going on in South Africa, very likely many things will be done there of which our sense would not altogether approve.

The war is over, but we have not exactly got peace. There is peace in Africa, but there is a little temporary disturbance existing in England. I find that the subject on which I have come to speak in Dublin this year is almost as controversial a subject as was the South African War. It is a very dull subject, but dull and dry though it be, it seems to excite the most furious passion.

I confess I feel very unequal to the task which I have been invited to perform. I feel as St Patrick must have felt when he landed to convert the Irish nation. I am told that the general opinion in this country is almost entirely against the view of economics which was usual six months ago, and I only hope that I may have, if not the good fortune St Patrick had, at any rate some proportion of that good fortune in driving out of Ireland the fiscal frogs and tariff toads.

I am very grateful to you for your kindness in allowing me to come here tonight and for the very friendly manner in which you have drunk my health. I am an excommunicated politician. My constituency has no confidence in me – they have said so several times, and they appear to derive the greatest satisfaction from repeating it; but a much more serious reverse has happened to me. Parliament is shortly to meet. The Tariff Commission was opened last week by Mr Chamberlain, and Parliament is to be opened next week by the King.

I have had no invitation to attend the Tariff Commission, and I have had no invitation to attend the Imperial Parliament. The customary letter which the Prime Minister sends to his supporters has on this occasion not been sent to one of his supporters. That is very sad, because I should greatly regret if I missed the opening of the Parliamentary Session, because I have several things I want very much to say.

So I hope if any of you should happen to see the date in the papers, and I should happen to forget, kindly write and let me know so that I may find my way there all the same. Now, gentlemen, you have certainly shown me a preference tonight, but it is not the sort of preference one would get under Protection.

I have certainly had something better to drink than Australian champagne, and I have not been invited to smoke the British North Borneo cigar, nor have I been offered snuff made out of Irish tobacco. I have been entertained in such a manner as leads me to believe that, concealed here and there amongst the audience I see before me, are a considerable number of the members of the Free Food League. At any rate I can assure you I am very grateful for the kindness and hospitality you have extended to me, and I shall carry away the most pleasant recollections of the Corinthian Club.

Winston Churchill

Of all our Prime Ministers Winston Churchill was probably the greatest diner and the greatest after-diner too. He was a considerable storyteller, though he was inclined to take the advice of Lord Brabazon of Tara, who said that if you couldn't say what you wanted to say in twenty minutes then you should write a book instead. Hence his four-volume *History of the English-Speaking Peoples,* which he described as 'our story', but which was a touch long for an 'after-dinner story' even for a nineteenth-century orator.

Occasionally, though not often, Churchill himself was the butt of some witticism from someone else. One such occasion was when, as a brash young minister, he cheekily poked Lord Haldane's pot-belly and asked the old boy what he was going to call it.

'If it's a boy, I shall call him George after His Majesty the

King,' said Haldane. 'If it's a girl, Mary after Her Majesty the Queen. But if it's only wind I shall call it Winston.'

There are also innumerable whisky-and-soda Churchill-isms. Or should I say, as he did, 'whisky and shoda'? Once he was given a very weak one at a diplomatic reception, whereupon he asked which had been put in first – the whisky or the shoda. 'Oh sir,' came the reply, 'I put in the whisky first.'

'Very good,' said Churchill. 'Then no doubt I shall come to it in due course!'

He often got a laugh for his insults. 'There but for the Grace of God goes God,' he once said of Stafford Cripps. When told by someone – and history claims that it was several different women including Nancy Astor and Bessie Braddock – that he was drunk, he replied ungallantly that this was true and that she was ugly. 'But in the morning I shall be sober!' When the Lord Privy Seal asked to see him while he was on the lavatory Churchill is supposed to have replied, 'Tell the Lord Privy Seal I am sealed to my privy, and can only deal with one shit at a time.'

'Pug' Ismay, his wartime Chief of Staff, once waded through an interminable memorandum and summed it up by scribbling one short word at the bottom. Then, when he realised that it was going up to the Prime Minister, he had second thoughts, crossed out the word and substituted 'Round Objects'.

Churchill's response was, 'Pray who is Mr Round and why does he object?'

One of his choicest insults was directed at his fellow Conservative Prime Minister, Stanley Baldwin. 'He occasionally stumbled over the truth,' said Winston, 'but hastily picked himself up and hurried on as if nothing had happened.' But Baldwin himself was no slouch when it came to the cutting phrase. It was he, after all, who once said, 'I met Curzon in Downing Street, from whom I got the sort of greeting a corpse would give to an undertaker.'

According to his biographer, Montgomery Hyde, Baldwin cultivated 'a slow conversational fireside manner suggesting that he was thinking aloud'. He himself had misgivings about allowing his speeches to be collected in printed form since they were 'in general delivered amidst the press of thronging duties and urgent preoccupations'. He was not much of a humorist but he appreciated the worth of humour. 'The English laugh', he said, quoting Ruskin, 'is the purest and truest in the metal that can be minted.' This was in his celebrated speech on England, delivered after dinner to the Royal Society of St George. The most sonorous passage is this:

On England

The sounds of England, the tinkle of the hammer on the anvil in the country smithy, the corncrake on a dewy morning, the sound of the scythe against the whetstone, and the sight of a plough team coming over the brow of a hill, the sight that has been seen in England since England was a land, and may be seen in England long after the Empire has perished and every works in England has ceased to function, for centuries the one eternal sight of England. The wild anemones in the woods in April, the last load at night of hay being drawn down a lane as the twilight comes on, when you can scarcely distinguish the figures of the horses as they take it home to the farm, and above all, most subtle, most penetrating and most moving, the smell of wood smoke

coming up in an autumn evening, or the smell of the scutch fires: that wood smoke that our ancestors, tens of thousands of years ago, must have caught on the air when they were coming home with the result of the day's forage, when they were still nomads, and when they were still roaming the forests and the plains of the continent of Europe. These things strike down into the very depths of our nature, and touch chords that go back to the beginning of time and the human race, but they are chords that with every year of our life sound a deeper note in our innermost being.

Stanley Baldwin

Baldwin was not slow in offering speech-making advice on delivery to others. After inviting the young A. P. Herbert to speak at the Worcestershire Society in 1928, he dropped him a line from Number 10.

Advice on speech-making

My dear A.P.H., I am going to risk being cut by you next time we meet and losing the Freedom of Hammersmith. But you are young and I am old and I am thinking of the future. I want you to take heed to the delivery of your speeches. It is at present without form and void. It is like an intermittent machine-gun fire, rapid but dropping at the end almost into inaudibility. Ordinarily this wouldn't matter but your stuff is A1. When you can put it over you will be in the top flight of after-dinner speakers. Study method. To my mind, at its best, Gordon Hewart is a model; every word and phrase tells. And so might your stuff: it is good enough but it doesn't get across properly. You may say, What business is it of yours? or Mind your own speeches. True, but you can be a first-class coach without being a first-class oar (Rudie Lehmann) and I can judge a speech. You have it in you to be so good and that is why I have butted in. That's all.

Stanley Baldwin

Herbert was grateful then and ever thereafter. 'What a wonderful thing,' he commented, 'that a Prime Minister should take the trouble to write so beneficent a letter to a young man he hardly knew! I glowed with gratitude, obeyed the advice and, I believe, improved.'

The absolute opposite of Baldwin – sprightly where Baldwin was stolid, mercurial where he was staid – Herbert was a famous wit in his day and much in demand for dinner. At the annual dinner of the Oxford University Society in 1928 his path collided with that of the choleric John Fothergill, a rum cove who kept the Spread Eagle pub in Thame near Oxford but who also occasionally catered at outside events. This is Fothergill's account, in his diary, of that auspicious occasion.

Falls of Lodore

The OUDS dinner in the Town Hall was 100 strong. The cook spoilt the black soup completely, curiously enough they all swallowed it – evidently they had sat down believing that the dinner was to be so good that this prejudice was strong enough to carry them through at least the first course of brownish salt lemonade. The next four courses were exquisite and the savoury sloppy. I was so disconsolate that I didn't dare to go through the screens into the room, though afterwards several of them, including Diccon Hughes, always generous, came round and thanked me for

John Fothergill

the best OUDS supper and the first where they had had enough to drink, which was clear. In the middle of A. P. Herbert's speech, when he was touching upon the coming Revolution, fifty of my best plates were dropped on the top of the fifty marble steps just outside the room, and as they clattered down with intermittent crashes he made full use of it, getting the laugh of the evening at my expense, though I admit that I myself thought of Southey's 'Falls of Lodore' at the same time.

Herbert was on the staff of *Punch* from 1924 to 1935, when he was elected Independent Member of Parliament for Oxford University. His wit was all the better for being barbed. An almost invariably funny speaker and writer, he was a great tilter at windmills and never more so than when having a go at the ass of a law. He wrote a brilliant series of 'Misleading Cases' in which he mocked the legal profession by invariably pitting it against a Mr Albert Haddock, a thinly disguised Herbert. Thus the *Board of Inland Revenue v. Haddock*, or *Rex v. Haddock*, in which Haddock is had up for attempting to pay his tax bill by cow rather than on a paper cheque. He wins. As well as being a professional funny man Herbert was also a considerable theorist, characteristically managing to be not only insightful about humour but also funny about it. Here he is addressing the English Association.

The English laugh

I am very proud to be standing here today as President of your famous and meritorious Association, even though like the may-fly I flutter in glory for a single day only. When I ask myself to what I am indebted for this honour I recall a true story – because I was there – of what happened during the journey of an Imperial Press Mission in New Zealand in 1925. Amongst other distinguished people there were Lord Burnham, Lord Astor, and a young man named Anthony Eden. At a state banquet in Wellington the Maori minister made a speech, a member of that fine and civilised race which did, they say, have certain cannibalistic tendencies in the past. 'Gentlemen have often asked me', said the Maori minister, 'to what I attribute my success in life. I tell them that my great-grandfather ate the first Presbyterian minister to land upon these shores; and I attribute my success in life to the Scottish blood in my veins.' That would be a very apposite story but for the fact that in my veins I have not got a single drop of Scottish blood.

I hope nobody will think of this address as a 'lecture', because a 'lecture' presupposes that the man speaking knows more than those he addresses on what he is talking about; and I certainly do not claim that I know more about laughter – even English laughter – than you do. Nor do I claim any sort of monopoly in laughter or in a sense of humour for the English race. Other races can also be quite funny, too. But it is true that we are especially proud and sensitive about what we call the British sense of humour. You may tell a man that he has no morals, or that he has no head for business, and he will not mind in the very least. He may even boast that he has no ear for music, that he cannot hum the tune of 'God Save the King' – though why he should boast of it I cannot think. But tell an Englishman that he has no sense of humour and he will knock you down. Harold Nicolson has quoted Lord Chesterfield as saying, 'Frequent laughter is the characteristic of folly and ill manners. It is the manner in which the mob express their silly joy in silly things. Laughter is a low and unbecoming thing.' Few of us would say that today. Then there was Goethe: 'One cannot have a sense of humour unless one be without conscience or responsibility.' That is a very severe and un-English judgment.

But there is some evidence that that is still the official view of fun. Years ago I used incautiously to deliver some lectures with the unfortunate title, 'On Being Funny'. They were delivered to learned Societies like this, and because they were supposed to be instructive and the Societies were 'non-profit-making', no entertainment tax had to be paid. One day at Bridlington, however, a Customs officer noticed the alarming title of the lecture and pricked up his ears. He reported the affair to headquarters at Billingsgate: and I then had a formal letter asking me to explain precisely what proportion of the lecture was entertaining and stating that no lecture in which more than one-third of the material was amusing could be regarded as educational.

There was a sad sequel to that. I was addressing an audience which included a party of schoolgirls, and I asked them when I told a funny story to be very careful not to laugh too much or their Society would have to pay entertainment tax. What was my horror to find that they took me seriously and sat in solemn silence throughout!

But undoubtedly the sense of humour, whether it is creditable or discreditable, is closely linked with our political character and qualities. One thing we boast of is our tendency to laugh when in danger. Harold Nicolson, to quote him again, has said, 'When faced with something menacing the English take instinctive refuge in a sense of humour.' I have often thought how disgusted Hitler must have been when, after he produced his terrible 'secret weapon', the V_1, we called it a 'doodle-bug', named after an American beetle. In the first war there was a picture of a Tommy with his rifle on his shoulder and with shells bursting round him, pausing to light his cigarette and saying, 'Arf a mo', Kaiser.' At the height of the Battle of Jutland an officer who was in the stokehold noticed two stokers talking busily together, and he wondered what they were saying to one another at that great moment. So he approached and he heard one of them say, 'Well, all I say is, he ought to have married the girl.'

Talking of 'doodle-bugs', there is a great story of Dame Lilian Braithwaite, now dead, who, at the time the 'doodle-bugs' were falling on London, was playing in *Arsenic and Old Lace* in a London theatre. When the 'doodle-bugs' came the company were not enjoying themselves quite so much, and there was some talk of leaving London and going on tour. 'Oh, yes,' said Dame Lilian, 'very well, let's go on tour. Where shall we go? Let's go to Dover.' So they stayed where they were, and the old lady used to cover herself up in the bathroom and hope for the best.

Those of you who know the theatre know that everybody concerned, if the takings on one Wednesday night are £300 and the following Wednesday only £290, is worried and depressed – they are '£10 down' – and proportionally elated if it is the other way. After one of the worst 'doodle-bug' nights the secretary came upon the old Dame sitting half-asleep and very cold in her dressing-gown. She woke her and said, 'Oh, Dame, did you have a terrible night?' The old lady drew herself up and said, 'No, indeed, we were £30 up.'

Then, of course, there is a second tendency – to laugh at ourselves. Although we as a nation are justly proud of our great Parliamentary institutions we often speak – and even did during the struggle – derisively of Parliament, calling it the 'gas works', the 'talking-shop', or any kind of oppro-brious epithet. This is put down to our 'sense of superior-ity'. Harold Nicolson wrote: 'Were their pride really to be humbled I do not believe the English would laugh any more loudly than the Germans or the Americans.' I am not so sure. Do you remember when France fell in 1940? Many, I remember, affected to be relieved, saying, 'Now we know where we are – no more damned Allies', and so on.

Then we do use our habit of laughter for a most important purpose, that is for the pricking of bubbles. I remember Winston Churchill saying of a very small but excitable gentleman who was in a passion about something, 'The honourable gentleman must try not to develop more steam than he is capable of containing.'

Two years ago I was in the Argentine and I heard some speeches by President Peron, whose oratorical technique, I am sorry to say, is rather akin to the Hitler technique. He will shout a few words – 'Abajo, los oligarchos!' – and then all the crowd will chant, 'Peron! Peron! Evita! Peron!', sometimes breaking into little songs. However, when the President opened our Conference of Authors and Composers of the World, he did so in a calm and admirable speech; but even then his countrymen thought fit to cry out, 'Peron! Peron! Evita! Peron!' Our excellent President, Mr Leslie Boosey, then said a few words: and at the end Mr William Walton thought that somebody should speak for Britain: so he shouted out from the back, 'Boo-sey! Boo-sey! Boo-sey!' which did not go down very well with anybody.

So it is clear that Fun is much mixed up with our political character and our most prized political virtues, a sense of proportion and a dislike of extremes. It is a matter for consideration what a difference it might have made to the history of the world if Hitler and that big man who runs the Russian State had been endowed with a little more sense of humour.

I suppose I must make some pretence to examine the Theory of Humour, but I am not, I hope, going to consider it too seriously or exhaustively. In the last war the Germans determined to take a lesson from our conduct in the First World War. You may remember that in the first war there was a man called Bairnsfather who did a lot of funny pictures of old soldiers. One of them showed an enormous hole in a wall at 'the front', and a young soldier saying to an old

soldier, 'What made that?': and the old soldier, who was fed up, said 'Mice.' Well, in the last war the Germans were determined to cultivate the glorious sense of humour which had helped the British troops to victory on so many occasions, so they gave this picture as an example of the kind of humour which had inspired the British; but, unfortunately, they had to add at the bottom, 'The hole was not really made by mice but by a shell.'

There is an old story of years ago that at a gathering of learned men, which was discussing what was 'the essence of humour', one said it was incongruity, another said it was misfortune, and others said this and that: but a lawyer who was not very fond of 'the world's foremost humorous journal' said, 'The essence of humour is surprise, and that is why you laugh when you see a joke in *Punch*.' But someone else, who was rather more fond of that paper than the other, said, 'Oh, no, the essence of humour is recognition; and that is why you laugh when you hear a joke in court.'

Mr Hazlitt, whose works I am sure you have all read,

described Man as 'the only animal that laughs and weeps, for he is the only animal that is struck by the difference between what things are and what they ought to be'. 'The essence of laughter', he said, 'is the incongruous, the disconnexion of one idea from another or the jostling of one idea against another.' That covers almost everything. It is very like the 'theory of misfortune', which is that every joke fundamentally is the joke of the old gentleman falling on a banana skin. If he is in a top-hat, you are a stage higher: and if, added to the banana skin and the top-hat, you have the Chancellor of the Exchequer on the way to present his Budget, you have, I suppose, the perfect 'humour of misfortune'.

But I do not like to think of humour in that light, because it must mean that humorists are men who batten on the misfortunes of the world. Of course, if that were true, they would not be alone. Doctors would not exist if there were not suffering; and lawyers would not exist if there were not disagreements: so that in Utopia, I suppose, there would be no doctors and no lawyers, and on this theory there would be no humorists.

Whatever is the answer to that, I think that to say that humour is based upon the perception of the difference between things as they are and things as they ought to be is pretty good. To this it must be added, of course, that any citizen is capable of such perception, but the humorist is one who can express the difference in a pithy and memorable phrase. This does mean that at least the best fun is a form of criticism. We now come to the tiresome argument about 'humour' and 'wit'. Cicero said that laughter is never far remote from derision. That may be true of wit, but not, I think, of humour. Harold Nicolson said that, whereas wit is always intentional, humour is always unintentional. I do not agree with that. Humour is more kindly, more humane, but it may be as much contrived and elaborate as wit. In humour we laugh at ourselves, at fate, and at circumstances; in wit we laugh at others.

Humour, perhaps, can be put into certain categories. There is first of all the 'obvious' – the banana skin, the false beard that falls, and so on. Secondly, we have the 'unexpected', such as the old story of the Duke of Devonshire who dreamt that he was making a speech in the House of Lords, woke up – and found that he was. A better story is that he had made a speech and someone said to him afterwards, 'Excuse me, your Grace, but it seemed to me that you were yawning once or twice in the course of your speech,' and he replied, 'Well, it was damned dull, wasn't it?'

Then there is the 'unintentional'. Parliament yields a great harvest of unintentional humour. There is one story about that great old lady, Eleanor Rathbone, a very fine person. Most of the women members are fine persons, but they do somehow have a way of making that very human assembly laugh in the wrong place. She was quoting statistics of maternal and infant mortality, before and after birth: and she said, at last, 'Mr Speaker, we have this ante-natal treatment and this post-natal treatment; and still we have these appalling figures.' The House, I believe, laughed for a long time. On another occasion Lady Astor was making one of her famous temperance speeches, and she spoke of the damage done by the alcohol drinkers to their stomachs, whereupon Mr Jack Jones, MP, said, 'I tell the noble and honourable lady that I will lay my stomach against hers any day.' I put that into *Big Ben* and it was the only line I have ever had censored; but, at the Lord Chamberlain's kindly suggestion, it went in in this form, 'I will bet my stomach against yours,' and got a big laugh every night, I don't quite know why. I remember in my early days in Parliament sitting in an all-night session and at 4 o'clock in the morning Willie Gallacher, that genial Communist, was making a speech. There was something funny about his voice, I thought, and it turned out that he was trying a new set of top dentures for the first time and they were not working very well. In the midst of his speech, a fierce denunciation of hard-hearted ministers, in the middle of a gesture, he said, 'Excuse me, Mr Speaker,' and took out his dentures and put them in his pocket – very brave, but richly comic.

Then there is the humour which depends upon the impossible. Innumerable stories could be quoted. One concerns a baby in a pram just inside a window on the ground floor. A burglar approaches and starts scratching at the window and making signs with the idea of suggesting to the baby that it should lift its hand and open the latch. The baby takes no notice for a time but at last it says, 'Don't be a damned fool, I can't walk yet.'

All these stories, such as they are, seem in some cases to be contrived and in some cases not, but they all depend on circumstances rather than words. Both kinds of joke may contain wisdom; and the best jokes do. One of my real favourites was told to E. V. Lucas by a Petty Officer in one of His Majesty's ships. I dare say you have heard it, but I like hearing me tell it, and as I am President of this body, you are going to hear it again. A very poor man had only sixpence in his pocket and he wanted a job. He saw an advertisement by the LCC for a post of lavatory attendant. He went for this job, and everything was going well when they found that he was unable to read or write – a qualification which, for reasons I cannot explain, is necessary for that particular occupation – I suppose for the filling up of forms. He still, however, had the sixpence in his pocket, and he was advised by a friend to put it on 'Love-lies-bleeding' in the 3.30, and, contrary to most human experience, the horse came in at 100 to 1. With his winnings he bought some vegetables and a cart, sold at a profit, bought more and sold again until at length he finished up as the head of a great multiple store with £50,000 to his credit – or rather, as he was a careful and old-fashioned man, in his stocking. He was asked, 'Why don't you go to the bank and put your money in the bank?' So he went and said to a bank-manager, 'Can I put £50,000 in your bank?' The bank-manager said, 'Well, we will see what we can do. Just write your name here, will you?' The man told him that he could not read or write. Even then the bank-manager was not deterred, and he said, 'Well, make your mark.' But then, much impressed, he said to him, 'Do you realise what a wonderful man you are? Here you are, a self-made man. You have built up this business from nothing; you have £50,000 to play with: and yet you cannot read or write! Have you ever thought, Mr Smith, what you might have been if you had been able to read or write?' 'Yes,' said Mr Smith, 'I should be a lavatory attendant.' That story contains a great philosophy of life, reminding us all that we need never give up hope.

I have got another story – a very silly story. [Here Sir Alan illustrated his story by drawing a diagram.] These two lines represent railway tracks crossing at right angles far out in the plain: and here is a signal-box where George, the signalman, looks after things. Here is a train coming at fifty miles an hour and it is fifty miles away. Here is another train coming at thirty miles an hour, and it is thirty miles away, and here is George ready to use the signals and to avert the kind of misfortune which you have already foreseen. Across the line is a little cottage where George lives with his poor, sick wife, who is in a bath-chair enjoying the setting sun. Here is Joe, the plate-layer, at the end of his day's work, coming to have a cup of tea with George. He goes up the steps to the signal-box and to his horror finds George lying dead over the levers. Joe knows all about those two trains which are approaching, but he does not know how to work the levers. So what does he do? He goes down the steps and across the lines, and he comes to where the old lady is in her chair, and he wheels her down to a different place and he says, 'Cheer up, old lady, you're going to see the finest bloody railway smash you ever saw in your life.'

Then I have jotted down a few things which have pleased me under the heading of wit. There is an old Irish saying, sometimes useful in debate. My father told me, when somebody says something at the end of an argument which shows that they have been wrong all the time, to say this in reply, 'The last thing you said is like the thirteenth stroke of a crazy clock which not only is itself discredited, but casts a shade of doubt over all previous assertions.'

There is the story of Whistler, who made some witty remark, and Oscar Wilde said, 'I wish I had said that,' whereupon Whistler said, 'You will, Oscar, you will.'

G. K. Chesterton said, 'The lights of Broadway would have been a paradise for a man who could not read.' A reference to the gaudy, flashing advertisements.

Of Sir Edward Carson there are some splendid stories. Cross-examining he said, 'I put it to you that you are a confirmed drunkard.' 'That's my business,' said the witness indignantly. 'Have you any other business?' asked Carson.

G. K. Chesterton said that journalists were people who were allowed to scribble on the back of advertisements. Somebody said that in the old days men had had the rack; now they have the Press.

J. M. Barrie was rather a shy man and yet he was always getting into the papers. It was thought that he disliked it very much, but all were not sure. It was said unkindly of him that he 'had a genius for stepping back into the lime-light'.

Then we have Shaw: 'The British soldier can stand up to anything except the British War Office.' There is the story of the American Slocum who, sailing round the world, came to St Helena. He wrote, 'The island is of volcanic origin. The British got it before it was cold.'

'A Prime Minister', someone said, 'has as much privacy as a goldfish.'

During the Irish troubles the Irish authorities put up a poster, 'Join the Constabulary and see the world', and the

IRA put up a poster next door, 'Join the police and see the next world.'

It was said of a statesman that he had sat on the fence so long that the iron had entered into his soul.

I remember on one occasion on the Green at Boston, Massachusetts, in the place where one would ordinarily find the simple notice, 'Keep off the grass', there were the words put up, 'Keep off the grass – if you want to roam, join the Navy.'

Then there is Augustine Birrell's reference to the House of Lords, 'who represent nobody but themselves and have the entire confidence of their constituents'.

I must not leave out Mr Belloc's addition to Goldsmith:

> Ill fares the land, to hastening ills a prey,
> Where wealth accumulates and men decay.

Belloc added:

> But how much more unfortunate are those
> Whose wealth declines and population grows!

Lord Hewart, the great Lord Chief Justice, now dead, complained once in a speech of the amount of time he had to spend in court listening to 'running-down cases'. He spent nearly all his days, he said, adjudicating on collisions between two stationary motor-cars, each on its right side of the road, and sounding its horn . . .

A. P. Herbert

Though Herbert is concerned with the English laugh, as far as one-liners go, I would be prepared to stick my neck out and say that the Americans have the edge here. Let us pause at this convenient spot to consider other aphorists who were masters and mistresses of the verbal dash rather than the oratorical plod. Consider, for example, the deliciously mischievous Mae West:

In brief

I always say keep a diary, and some day it will keep you.

A man in the house is worth two in the street.

When you think about it, what other playwrights are there besides O'Neill, Tennessee and me?

I used to be Snow White, but I drifted.

Mae West

Then there were the famous wits of the Algonquin Round Table in the 20s and 30s, stalwarts, for the most part, of the *New Yorker* magazine and all aphorists rather than story-tellers. It was Robert Benchley, for example, who, on arriving in Venice, sent the famous telegram: STREETS FULL OF WATER. PLEASE ADVISE. Coming out of a nightclub into the rain one night he tapped a uniformed figure on the shoulder and said: 'Get me a cab.' The uniformed figure turned round furiously and informed him that he was not a doorman but a rear admiral. 'OK,' said Benchley, 'get me a battleship.' Benchley's friend and fellow *New Yorker* scribe (they

shared an office so small that Benchley commented ('One square foot less and it would be adulterous') was Dorothy Parker, unsurpassed when it came to wordplay: she could produce double and triple entendres with the skill the Yankees or Dodgers brought to baseball. Who else could have come up with 'You can bring a whore to culture but you can't make her think'? Or how about:

In brief

One more drink and I'd have been under the host.

On Katherine Hepburn at a Broadway first night: She ran the whole gamut of emotions from A to B, and put some distance between herself and a more experienced colleague lest she catch acting from her.

This is not a novel to be tossed lightly aside. It should be thrown with great force.

All I need is room enough to lay a hat and a few friends.

The affair between Margot Asquith and Margot Asquith will live as one of the prettiest love stories in all literature.

That woman speaks eighteen languages and she can't say No in any of them.

Dorothy Parker

One of the greatest wise-crackers of them all was Groucho Marx. His ancestors, he was fond of saying, 'came over on the *Mayflower*, having missed the *Augustflower*'. Egged on by their mother, Minnie – who said of showbusiness:

'Where else can people who don't know anything make so much money?' – Groucho and his brothers improvised and ad-libbed their way from vaudeville to Broadway and thence to Hollywood. 'We played towns I would refuse to be buried in today,' he said, 'even if the funeral were free and they tossed in a tombstone.' Groucho's flippancies were, on his own admission, 'oft-repeated' – in letters, on screen, in articles and interviews, and no doubt before, during and after dinner. Like Mae West and Dorothy Parker, many of his most memorable remarks concerned the battle between the sexes: even at his first wedding, when the Justice asked, 'Do you take this woman to be your lawful wedded wife?' he retorted, 'We've gone this far, we may as well go through with it . . .' Discovered kissing the maid, he said: 'I was just whispering in her mouth.' 'I was married by a judge,' he said later; 'I should have asked for a jury.'

In brief

A man's only as old as the woman he feels.

Time wounds all heels.

Marriage is a wonderful institution . . . but who wants to live in an institution?

Will you marry me? Do you have any money? Answer the second question first.

I've been around so long, I knew Doris Day before she was a virgin.

Behind every successful man there is a woman, behind her is his wife.

Groucho Marx

What he really wanted, as this wonderful extended piece of lunacy demonstrates, was a *femme fatale* . . .

How to be a spy

On becoming a spy, you will have to learn to deal with feminine wiles. The temptation of a beautiful woman can be your downfall – if you're lucky. Of course, Marx, the Master Spy, is proof against blandishments of the sveltest brunettes and the most ravishing blondes on earth. On the other hand, a redhead can get anything out of me in two minutes flat.

Let me tell you about my first *femme fatale*, that suave, bejeweled agent of Hungroslavia. Her name was Mandolin, and I shall always remember that evening in her scented boudoir on the Rue de la Strapontin-Casace. My mission was to wrest from her the blueprints of the fearsome Gatling gun . . .

But I am getting ahead of my story. Let me tell you how the mission first started. Our spy outfit was stationed on a secret island off the French coast. We had all been through a terrifying period: we had run out of paper clips, and we could no longer file reports in sextuplicate. We had to have clips! One panic-stricken soul among us suggested we try a clip joint, but that would have been tantamount to dealing in the black market. I was running feverishly all over the island. I was ready to drop in my tracks, except that I don't run on tracks.

Then the General approached me. 'Marx,' he said, 'you must go to the mainland in a small, unseaworthy craft and then proceed to Paris on a small, ungroundworthy motor-cycle. Once there you must wrest the blueprints of the fearsome Gatling gun from the beauteous Mandolin. May you wrest in peace.'

I set out at midnight in a dory. The waves were so high that they broke over the gunwales (pronounced gunnels). All I could find to bail with was a funwale (pronounced fun-nel). To make matters worse, the night was black as a tunwale (pronounced tunnel). This kind of humor is known as beating a dead horse, so let's drop it.

Suffice to say, I eventually reached Paris and burst in upon the beauteous Mandolin. 'Dear lady,' I said as I took her in my arms, 'I am not hemmed to fit the touch of your skirt!' (This is the way spies always talk to each other – code language.)

'Mandolin,' I continued, 'I have come to curry favor.' I ran my fingers through her hair. 'Sorry I forgot my curry-comb.' Then I prostrated myself before her. 'Mandolin,' I slavered. 'I swear that your beauty has crazed me. Your eyes, how they shine! They shine like the pants of a blue serge suit!'

At that moment the plans of the Gatling gun dropped from her bodice – I snatched them.

'Monster!' she shrieked. 'For this night's work you shall reap dismay!'

'You've got it all wrong,' I said. 'I shall plow dismay – I won't be reaping till dis-august.'

At that point Mandolin's lover, the Count de la Défense d'Afficher, rushed into the room. I had to swallow the blueprints quick, and I must say they were the worst I've ever tasted.

'*Cochon!*' cried the Count. 'What are you doing in my fiancée's apartment?'

'Well, right now I'm trying to find a bicarbonate of soda.'

He advanced and slapped me across the cheek with his gloves. I could not let this challenge go unheeded. I produced my card-case. 'Take one, Monsieur,' I snapped.

He did.

'What is it?' I said.

'Queen of spades.'

'Pay me – I drew the ace.'

This did not satisfy him, however, so I stalked away to my motorcycle and drove off in low dudgeon – I couldn't make high on the gasoline we were getting in those days.

Groucho Marx

W. C. Fields aptly remarked once: Groucho was 'the only act I could never follow'.

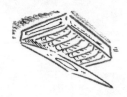

The English equivalent of the Algonquin Round Table was, for years, the weekly *Punch* table, but for epigrammatic dottiness of the most English sort I prefer the actor/writer Sir Herbert Tree and his wife, Lady Tree. In his wonderfully funny but now neglected autobiographical *Great Morning*, Osbert Sitwell recalls them.

Sir Herbert and Lady Tree

Singly or together, Sir Herbert and Lady Tree could be depended upon to supply an entertainment of the most delicious personal fantasy, based on the flimsiest and most delicate foundation of sense. Though I, with the rest of the world, have seen quoted and heard repeated so many of Sir Herbert's remarks and exploits – as, when, for example, he went to a post-office and asked for a penny stamp, and on being given one, demanded, 'Have you no others?', and, after a sheet of them had been produced, considered it exhaustively, head by head, and then, selecting a stamp in the very middle, pointed at it, and remarked with decision,

'I will take that one'; and though, equally, I have read, heard, or been told of many of Lady Tree's epigrams, such as when, being offered two kinds of fish at a dinner-party, she remarked, 'Ye cannot serve both Cod and Salmon', or when – another ichthyophagous bon-mot – on a similar occasion haddock was handed to her, and she exclaimed joyously 'Cry "Haddock!", and let slip the dogs of war', yet nothing can do justice to the captivating absurdity with which they both invested everyday life.

Osbert Sitwell

Even on her deathbed Lady Tree managed a witticism. Realising the end was nigh she summoned her lawyer in order to make some last-minute adjustments to her will and, when he arrived, announced to her grieving relations, 'My darlings, here comes my solicitor, to teach me my Death-Duties.'

But I digress, just as, I may say, A. P. Herbert was inclined to do when public speaking. Let us return to the master. Where was he? Ah yes . . .

The English laugh – again

There are at least two departments in which we excel; one is nonsense. It is extraordinary that the staid Victorians should have produced two such nonsense-makers as Lewis Carroll and Edward Lear. Mr Harold Nicolson said of nonsense that 'it might not be an index of a very active intellect but it is an index of a most agreeable temperament'. Our capacity for nonsense is rather an endearing aspect of our character.

The other department is parody. I am sorry Sir John Squire, who was to have taken the Chair on this occasion, is not here, because there we have a master of that important art. Max Beerbohm you have all read. My old chief, Owen Seaman, was a very good parodist. Parody is not as easy as it looks.

Then, of course, there is graphic fun, funny pictures. Here I should like to make a slight private and indiscreet complaint. It used to be the fashion to run down the old pictures in Punch with their long conversations and explanations at the foot. But now everything has gone the other way and we have just pictures, which may or may not be intelligible, and no words. That may be a better form of art, but what grieves me is this, that no longer are the funny papers, whether Punch or the New Yorker, in their pictures mirrors of the times. When we want to do a play of the period 1870 we can go to Punch and we know exactly when

crinolines went out and the bustle came in, and we see some very nice-looking people of the period. But if anybody in the year AD 2000 proposed to make a play about this present time he would get very little out of *Punch* or the *New Yorker*. He would get no idea what people looked like. Most of the women indeed look like halfwits or hyenas, and it is not until you turn to the advertisement pages of the *New Yorker* that you see the luscious young ladies who restore your faith in the human race. I do think that it is a pity that the comic draughtsmen have gone so far from the Victorian methods.

Then the humour of the people. You cannot meet anybody in any walk of life who has not got a funny story, sometimes very good. How many have I produced today? I did not make up the stories I have told you. Lord knows where they came from or who produced them. Some say they are produced on the Stock Exchange. If so, the people concerned ought to be earning a lot more money a lot more easily by writing humorous plays. You never meet a man who says, 'I made up that funny story,' but the stories go round like Homer, unwritten, unrecorded.

If I have not delayed you too long I should like to say a few words about our richness of local fun. We have got the Irish and Scotch with their peculiar brand of humour, or rather our peculiar brand of humour about them. And we have the Welsh. I shall never allow anybody to say that the Welsh have no sense of humour after what happened to me on one occasion. I had spent a very bad holiday in Wales. It rained all the time and I came back in a bad temper, and wrote some lines to the tune of 'Land of My Fathers'. One day a man spoke to me in the House of Commons and said, 'I am in an awful fix. Saturday is St David's Day and Mr Lloyd George was going to come to speak to us, but he is down with the "flu".' So I said jocularly that I would come. To my horror he took me seriously and I had to go and deputise for Mr Lloyd George on St David's Day. I, too, had a bad cold and before that Welsh audience I husked into the microphone the following unworthy song:

Wales! Wales! land of the slugs and the snails!
In buckets and pails
The rain falls on Wales
And when it's not raining
It hails.

And that Welsh audience laughed and laughed and ap-
plauded; so that they must have a sense of humour in Wales.

A. P. Herbert

. . . Forgive me for butting in again on Mr Herbert but I cannot pass up this opportunity to tell another Welsh tale I recently heard when invited to sing for my supper by telling tallish stories to passengers on board the cruise ship *Caronia*. This one was told by Dennis Morgan, a retired History lecturer from Cardiff, who kept his dinner-table in stitches with stories ancient and modern, delivered in the sort of Welsh accents which have kept countless pews of Valley Methodists mesmerised by preachers in chapel pulpits for hundreds of years. It goes something like this:

The Russians were attempting to set up a spy ring in Wales. A top KGB agent called (of course) Vladimir was told, 'Proceed to Cardiff and take the branch line to Abercwmscwt. There you will meet a man called Jones. You will say to him, "The daffodils are blooming early this year." He will reply, "Yes, but the tulips are late." He will tell you how to set up the spy ring.'

Vladimir finally arrives at Abercwmscwt and asks the ticket collector, 'Do you know a man called Jones?' The ticket collector replies, 'Well, it depends which Jones you want. There's Jones the Bread, Jones the Milk, Jones the Death (he's the funeral director). In fact, my name is Jones.' 'The daffodils are blooming early this year,' says Vladimir. 'Oh,' says the ticket collector, 'it's Jones the spy you want.'

Dennis says this is a classic example of the place of gossip in a Welsh village.

Singing for one's supper can sometimes be a literal requirement of after-dinner entertaining. The agonies that may ensue are memorably described by Jane Austen in *Pride and Prejudice*, when Elizabeth Bennet's sister Mary takes to the piano at the Netherfield Ball. Her 'powers were by no means fitted for such a display; her voice was weak, and her manner affected.' It is an enormous relief to one and all when her father steps in with the famous words: 'That will do extremely well, child. You have delighted us long enough.'

Similarly Lady Lawless, the British Ambassadress in Rome in Maurice Barings' novel, C, knew exactly how to deal with such situations:

Such a treat

'I like that one best of all,' she said, 'and *how* kind of you to have been able to spare us a moment tonight, and to have given us *all such* a treat, and to have sung *so* many songs. I do hope it hasn't *tired* you; you must take care of that precious throat. The Ambassador has so enjoyed it; we *all* have, and you must come to tea and sing another song very soon.' And as she talked she took Miss Sim's music from the pianoforte, and rolled it up neatly in a rouleau, and tied it with a little piece of pink ribbon, and presented it to her with a charming and completely final bow, and calling Herbert Napier she said to him, 'Mr Napier, will you take Miss Sims to have a cup of tea and some lemonade?' And so saying, she led the guests back to the drawing-room, and Napier conducted Miss Sims to a small buffet on the top of the staircase, where there were refreshments, whence she was ultimately shown out.

'She may do for concerts in England,' said Lady Lawless. 'One never knows what English people will like.'

Maurice Baring

But let us return to A. P. Herbert and hear how he ended his review of the English laugh . . .

The English laugh – chorus

I regret that no longer have we the old comic songs. This seems to be a lost art. One song comes into my mind:

> There was I, waiting at the church,
> > waiting at the church,
> > > waiting at the church,
> When I found he'd left me in the lurch
> Lor! how it did upset me . . .
> All at once they handed me a note,
> This is what he wrote –
> Here's the very note:
> 'I can't get away to marry you today,
> My wife won't let me.'

Some of these songs are, in their words, of incredible brutality, but somehow they never give you the real sense of brutality. They have a friendly and genial air.

Then there is another branch of humour – the practical joke. Thank goodness, we do not see much of them. I had a frightful experience after giving a lecture in Copenhagen. My speech went down pretty well, but next day I saw my name in the headlines of the papers and I asked a Copenhagen lady whom I was sitting next to at lunch what it was about, and she said, 'It seems you are a very good practical joker, Mr Herbert.' To my horror I found that all the famous practical jokes committed by Mr Cole, a well-known practical joker, had been ascribed to me personally: the joke about pretending to be a road repairer and taking up half Piccadilly and diverting the traffic – challenging Sir John Simon to run a hundred yards down Piccadilly in a certain time, giving him my stop-watch and when he started, crying 'Stop thief! He's got my watch!' – the joke about pretending to be a surveyor, giving a measuring tape to one man, walking round a corner and giving the other end to another, and then leaving them both standing – you can imagine my feelings when I saw all these things put down personally to me.

Ladies and gentlemen, thank you for your forbearance. Whether you are any wiser on account of what I have said I doubt, but I think you will agree that laughter is good for us. It is good for the body, they say, because it empties the lungs and helps to circulate the blood, and it is certainly good for the soul. When we laugh, richly and gloriously, without restraint and bitterness, we forget ourselves and the world and we are as angels looking down on life, laughing at it but loving it. And we humble people who try to earn a living as humorous writers are proud and privileged to think that now and then, if we are successful, we can make you laugh and cause a little happiness.

A. P. Herbert

There's no doubt that A. P. Herbert was good on his feet. He was also a great writer of verse – the sort who would break into rhyme at the drop of a hat, reeling off the rollicking couplets to the entertainment of all and sundry. Before we leave him, here's some verse he wrote about a dinner where, for once, the ladies seem to have remained for the port and he appears to have taken quite a shine to the girl next to him . . . It's called, simply, 'After dinner'.

After dinner

I will not make a speech tonight,
I have not had sufficient wine;
It is not just, it is not right
To ask a fellow out to dine
And treat him in this kind of way –
I WILL not make a speech, I say.

No, Mr Secretary, NO!
Ask Mr Mudd to say a word,
Let Mr Mumble have a blow –
He is not happy, I have heard,
Except when he is on his feet
Extemporising after meat.

But I am very dumb tonight;
I cannot think of words at all;
My neighbour's eyes are very bright,
My neighbour's hands are very small,
And if I did say something, Sir,
I fancy it would be to her.

The wine was good (though I repeat,
I have not had enough of it);
I liked the fish, I liked the sweet,
The company is exquisite;
And that's exactly what I feel
About this admirable meal.

And you are free to write it down
And put it in the minute-book,
And I will give you half-a-crown
And you can give it to the cook –
But damned be he who here suggests
That I should answer for The Guests!

My neighbour's eyes are very bright,
My neighbour's hands are very small,
And I am very gay tonight;
O Mercy, must we spoil it all?
A speech is long but life is short,
Please go away – and pass the port.

A. P. Herbert

Ladies and gentlemen, one knows the feeling.

One woman who told stories in public at the same time and with as much aplomb as A. P. Herbert was Joyce Grenfell. Although the piece which follows is strictly an after-tea rather than an after-dinner piece, it conforms to all the demands of the classic after-dinner genre.

I remember, after I had written an adulatory piece about Joyce, a distinguished fellow journalist telephoned and asked why I had been so soft on her. I was bemused. Why should I be hard on her? As Richard Garnett said in a tribute to her after her death, she was that rare thing – a person both good and 'unboring'. He described her answering a question at a literary luncheon on how she became an entertainer:

'She was away. It was beautifully done: impromptu, just enough of a performance to make it entertaining, but not to destroy the easy intimacy of a conversation among friends. They loved it. They loved her.'

Clive James tells how the Sydney University Journalists' Club invited her for lunch, convinced that she would refuse. She said yes. On the appointed day they lined up to greet her 'looking like a firing squad in mufti'. Towards the end of lunch:

'Joyce chose a pear, decapitated it, and rotated her spoon inside it, extracting the contents undamaged, whereupon the empty skin fell contentedly inwards. It was all done with inexpressibly accomplished ease ... While we sat with mouths ajar, she whipped an Instamatic out of her reticule and photographed us.'

This 'after-tea speech' was Joyce Grenfell's debut in Herbert Farjeon's *Little Revue*, which opened at the Little Theatre, London, on 21 April 1939, and went on to run for 415 performances. It began life on the same day on which she met Stephen Potter for the first time, so let us allow him to introduce it:

'At last Potters met Grenfells in the house of friends. Joyce had heard that morning in the country a woman speaking at a village institute, one of those nice bright people whose advice is so helpful but yet whose cheerfulness casts a chill. Joyce described the woman, and then suddenly and naturally *became* the woman. That was the shock. I stared at Joyce. She was talking about acceptable gifts . . .'

Useful and acceptable gifts

Madam President, Fellow Institute Members, good even- ing. This evening I am going to tell you a little bit about my useful and acceptable gifts, and these gifts are not only easy to make but ever so easy to dispose of. I see several of you ladies have your eye on the boutonnière in my lapel – it *is* pretty, isn't it? – and I am going to tell you how to make one just like it. First of all you must obtain some empty beech- nut husk clusters. These are to be found beneath beech trees almost any time after about the middle of September onwards. Cleanse your husks thoroughly. And then wire them on to stalks or stems. (You will find six or eight are ample for a boutonnière.) Now, before you *colour* you must decide what flower it is you are making. Mine are wood anemones – shell-pink without, and a deeper rose within. (Sometimes I like to use just a *suspicion* of gold or silver! I like to feel that we take Nature's gifts and make them even lovelier.) Now, when you are making beech-nut husk flowers do not confine yourself to boutonnières. *Be bold* about it! You can make great sprays of lupes, or delphs. (If anybody wants to take notes I shan't mind a bit.)

Well, next we come to a more serious gift – waste-paper baskets, or should I say more accurately – waste-paper bas- kets, for they are made from manufacturers' biscuit tins, and in order to obtain these you must make love to your grocer and wheedle him into giving one to you. First, cleanse your tin thoroughly and then remove all existing advertising matter. In order to obtain my unusual mosaic design you are going to want some pieces of wallpaper patterns. (I prefer beige tones myself.) Tear your paper up into scraps – the smaller the better – and then paste the pieces all over the *outside* of the tin – higgledy-piggledy, in what you might call a crazy-paving design; and when the pieces are quite firm, outline them in black Indian ink, and you will find you have not only a useful waste-paper basket, but a very unusual piece of modernistic furniture as well.

So much for tins. And lastly we come to what I like to call my comic turn! Dicky Calendars – Dicky Calendars. Dicky is made from two india-rubbers, or, as we called them when I went to school, bunjies! You will want a small one for the head and a strong sturdy one for the body. The head must be joined *to* the body, so obtain some strong wire and pass it through the head and right through poor Dicky's body to emerge as his legs. Mount him on a cardboard paper stand, give him two bright pin eyes and a pheasant or chicken's feather for a tail, and then, with a calendar on a jaunty ribbon round his neck, Dicky is ready to keep you up to date!

Ladies, it is our duty as women to beautify our surroundings. Now when you get home I want you to seek out materials to make yourself Useful and Acceptable Gifts. Good evening.

Joyce Grenfell

Joyce Grenfell was famously funny on her feet and in song. Evelyn Waugh, one of the twentieth century's funniest storytellers, was better in print. He did, however, produce a memorable off-the-cuff remark about his contemporary, the impossible Randolph Churchill, after surgeons had operated on him: 'A triumph of modern science', he said, 'to find the only part of Randolph that wasn't malignant and remove it.' Generally, however, Waugh needed to be read rather than listened to, as he himself was disarmingly aware. Here he is in his diaries recalling a speech at the Royal Naval College, Greenwich.

Dreading it

On Tuesday 31 Jan. Laura and I separated after breakfast, she to drive home, I to take the train to London where I had to dine and speak at the Staff College at Greenwich, an engagement I made months ago for the insufficient reason that the secretary wrote such a pleasant letter of invitation. For weeks I had been dreading it. We left Brighton in warm sunshine. Before I reached London snow was falling. I went to White's which was full and jolly. A *mot* of Andrew Devonshire's: Randolph boasted he was going to Washing-

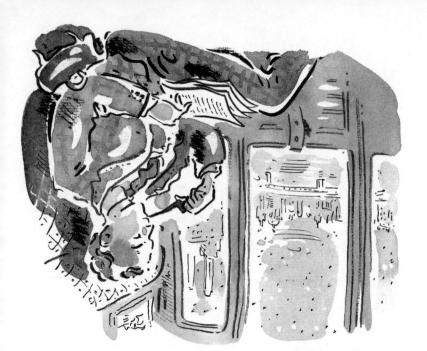

ton 'to keep Jerk in order'. 'Ah,' said Andrew, 'the last camel to break the straw's back.' I invited myself to lunch at the Savile with Peters and my American publisher – a dull dog. There was an aged, snowy-haired, grey-faced, shabby man opposite me who did not look like anyone I had ever seen before. Peters said, 'Have you quarrelled with Peter Rodd?' It was he . . . The Greenwich evening was quite enjoyable. Half an hour's heavy enforced drinking in the anteroom, then dignified dinner in the Painted Hall. Then we adjourned to the anteroom where I spoke for half an hour. I don't know what I said, nor I am sure did my audience – a small club of senior officers – but it seemed to be a success. Then an hour of heavy enforced drinking.

Evelyn Waugh

Waugh was, of course, an Oxford man. Hence *Brideshead Revisited*. He was socially handicapped by only making it to Hertford and not to Christ Church, the college to which he aspired. He took his revenge by introducing a character in his novels called Crutwell (after the Dean of Hertford) and making sure that he was not one of the stars of the show. Witty man though he was, Waugh eschewed speaking at Balliol's Arnold and Brackenbury Society, rejecting the invitation by saying that 'he could not come to the Society's dinner and that the Society would not like it if he did'.

Gerard Hoffnung, on the other hand, created his comedy out of an affected disdain for his audience's expectations, most memorably perhaps in 1958 when he addressed the Oxford Union. His address was nominally on the subject of the importance of supporting music and the arts, and was, luckily for us, recorded by the BBC. It took the form of a somewhat surrealist autobiography – a father who was a zookeeper, an aunt with a passion for brass bedknobs – and involved letters written to him while working at the Ministry of Pensions:

'Sir, I have been in bed with the doctor for a week and it doesn't seem to be doing me much good ... Should I get another doctor?'

'Sir, this is to notify you that I have given birth to twins in the enclosed envelope ...'

'Re your dental enquiry: the teeth in the top are doing fine, but the ones in my bottom are hurting terribly.'

And the following replies in response to holiday enquiries to various hoteliers in the Dolomites:

'In the close village you can buy jolly memorials for when you pass away ...'

'I am amazing diverted by your entreaty for a room. I can offer you a commodious chamber with a balcony imminent to a romantic gorge, and I hope you will want to drop in.'

'I am not too good in bath, but I am superb in bed.'

'Sorrowfully I cannot abide your auto.'

'Standing among savage scenery, the hotel offers stupendous revelations. There is a French widow in every bed-room, affording delightful prospects.'

'Our motto is "ever serve you right." ...'

The most hilarious and unforgettable story of all, however, now a classic, was the one on the improbable subject of the

laying of bricks. Much, alas, is lost in the telling on the printed page, but try to imagine the whole episode delivered in portentously tragic tones, interrupted throughout with helpless mirth as the audience anticipates the inevitable next stage. When Hoffnung says, 'At this point I must have lost my presence of mind', the house comes down. Here it is, then: a letter from a bricklayer in Golders Green to the company for which he works.

From a bricklayer in Golders Green

RESPECTED SIR,

When I got to the top of the build-ing, I found that the hurricane had knocked some bricks off the top.

So I rigged up a beam with a pulley at the top of the building, and hoisted up a couple of barrels of bricks. When I had fixed the building there *was* [emphasis] a lot of bricks left over.

I hoisted the barrel back up again and secured the line at the bottom. I went up to the top and filled the barrel with extra bricks. Then I went to the bottom and cast off the line.

Unfortunately . . . the barrel of bricks was heavier than I was and before I knew what was happening the barrel started down – jerking me off the ground.

I decided to hang on. And halfway up I met the barrel coming down, and received severe blows on the shoulder.

[Pause . . . giggle.]

I then continued to the top – banging my head against the beam and getting my fingers jammed in the pulley.

When the barrel hit the ground it burst its bottom, allowing all the bricks to spill out.

I was now heavier than the barrel and so started down again at high speed.

Halfway down, I met the barrel coming up and received severe injuries to my shins. When I hit the ground, I landed on the bricks, getting several painful cuts from the sharp edges.

At this point I must have lost my presence of mind, because I let go the line . . .

The barrel . . . the barrel, the barrel then came down, giving me another heavy blow and putting me in hospital.

I respectfully request sick leave.

Gerard Hoffnung

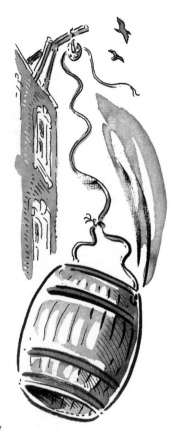

Hoffnung was one of those rare birds who obviously made you laugh before he had even opened his mouth. He had a funny presence, a funny voice and perhaps above all an exquisite sense of timing. His wife Annetta described his wholehearted enthusiasm as 'his most endearing, infuriating and remarkable characteristic'. On the other hand I am uneasily aware that some of his funniest moments were in front of an audience at the Oxford Union, and that tends to raise hackles. 'Undergraduate humour', I hear critics mutter alongside a sort of groundswell of class resentment other-wise reserved for Eton. Perhaps Balliol is even worse. You all know the rhyme about one of Balliol's effortlessly resentable sons, the one whom Baldwin compared with a corpse:

My name is George Nathaniel Curzon,
I am a most superior person,
My cheek is pink, my hair is sleek,
I dine at Blenheim twice a week.

I don't know if Curzon made speeches after his twice weekly Blenheim dinners, but if he did I bet the more he looked down his aristocratic nose the more he got up the noses of his audience. This would certainly have been true if any non-Balliol men had been in the college hall the night Harold Macmillan addressed us in his role as Chancellor. I particularly remember him saying with mock surprise that one of the best things about becoming Chancellor of Ox-ford was that he discovered that, contrary to what he had always supposed in a long Balliol life, there were other col-leges in Oxford, many of them quite agreeable. There was even one next door called Trinity, with a surprisingly pretty garden. And so on.

Macmillan was patron saint of the nearest I have discov-ered to a school for after-dinner speaking (of a particular sort), which is the Arnold and Brackenbury Society. Until 1955 it traded under two separate identities – the Arnold, named after Matthew, a distinguished old boy of the college, and Brackenbury, named after Hannah, one of its great benefactresses. The two societies seem to have had pretensions to seriousness and the Arnold was much given to play-reading.

For much of its history, however, and certainly since 1955, it has been a sort of frivolous debating society, nearly always debating after dinner, and invariably after drink. The motions themselves give the flavour: 'This house prefers bedroom farce to Attic drama'; 'This house would raise Cain if it were Abel'; 'This house would rather be effortless than superior'; 'This house would bury the rock of ages below the sands of time'.

Some of the most elegantly caustic minutes were penned by Tom Bingham, later Lord Chief Justice, and Martin Hammond, now headmaster of Tonbridge School. It was Hammond who recorded of the future Governor of Hong Kong, 'Mr Patten told another of his stories; this time about Lancelot, Arthur, Merlin, a dragon in Bodmin and water on the knee, which sounded like a rejected script for *Camelot*.' Bingham wrote of his friend, later Sir John Keegan, the distinguished military historian and analyst, 'The retiring President, Mr Keegan, made a farewell speech which was moving, but not fast enough.'

In 1969 the Secretary reported unkindly of the former Master, 'Sir David is an old friend of the Society and so is his speech.' Sir Patrick Mayhew MP, a former President, once complimented the Society on the permanence of its values. 'It could be relied on to applaud the same jokes year after year,' reported the Secretary, adding that this was 'a fact which Mr Mayhew then proceeded to take advantage of.' One guest 'brought greetings from another society and made a speech which left one thankful that he had come alone'.

Members were taught that extreme rudeness may not be funny but often induces laughter. Lord David Cecil, invited over from New College to speak after dinner in 1960, observed that it was 'an intellectual bloodbath' and said that 'he had never felt so inferior except in a women's college'.

Which reminds me incidentally of this story about Cecil told by his former pupil, now the distinguished theatre director, Patrick Garland.

Lord David Cecil's dismay

Although he later became a much loved tutor when I went up to Oxford in the late 1950s, my first glimpse of Lord David Cecil happened when I was still a schoolboy, watching television. This was in the old black and white days, during a programme which just about survives late at night on Radio Three when nobody's listening, called 'The Brains Trust'. Then, it was a commonplace weekly programme on Prime Viewing. The usual group sat in front of the immobile cameras: Professor Alan Bullock, Marghanita Laski, Michael Ayrton, Lord David Cecil, Sir Malcolm Sargent. Under discussion that evening – 'Was it true, the youth of the present day were worse behaved, less educated, more untidy than the youth of the previous generation?' The distinguished panel were in unanimous agreement: yes, the youth of the present generation were, indeed, worse behaved, less educated, etc. etc.

'What is your opinion, Lord David Cecil?' asked the Question Master. Lord David illustrated his agreement and dismay with this personal anecdote:

'I was in the Randolph Hotel, in my home city of Oxford, only the other week,' he began, 'walking down the central staircase to Reception, when I saw advancing up the stairs towards me the most unusual apparition. He seemed in dreadful disarray. His hair was unbrushed and his tie undone. There was a scattering of white powder on his collar and his waistcoat buttons were fastened unevenly. His trousers seemed to be stretched upwards, there was a gap between his turn-ups and his ankles. His shoe-leather was, alas, unpolished and fly buttons undone. As we approached one another on the stairs, I thought to myself: "Oh dear; standards are falling." Ladies and gentlemen, I was looking in a mirror.'

Patrick Garland

Cambridge University also produces after-dinner speakers. Of course it does. They have a debating Union, they have the Footlights, and they have the college smokers – after-dinner entertainments par excellence. Clive James, who was offered the daunting honour of directing the Pembroke smoker in the wake of Peter Cook's famed tenancy, describes his first attempt.

The Pembroke smoker

I was talked out of my gloom and into the job. Actually, the show couldn't lose. Eric Idle was in it and he knew all the ropes. Above all, he knew that what really mattered was the wine. Into Pembroke's old library, called Old Library, were carried many boxes of a cheap but acceptably smooth Beaujolais from Peter Dominic, who also supplied the glasses. Many of these were broken on the first night by the Hearties. The show ran for four nights and everybody came.

The Hearties were merely the noisiest element. Large, boat-rowing types with low foreheads, thick necks and annoyingly pretty female companions imported from London, they laughed at everything, including the love songs. Everyone else enjoyed the show too, although most of them would have been hard put to give a clear account of it afterwards. All the men were in black tie and all the women in evening gowns. Some of the male dons would have liked to have been in evening gowns also, but they confined themselves to lip-stick and rouge. The stage, constructed from beer-crates for the occasion, was only about six feet square and stood uncur-tained in one corner of the room, so that you could make an entrance through the door leading to the book-stack. The rest of the room was packed with small low tables tightly sur-rounded by increasingly happy people. The oxygen was quickly used up. So was the wine, except that our waiters kept replacing it. The heat was terrific. Breathing neat nitro-gen, with only an unlimited supply of plonk to stave off dehydration, the entire audience was already drunk before the lights went down on the first act. Even the dons were shouting. But the level of physical behaviour remained decorous if you didn't count the periodic attempts by the Hearties to smash their table by dancing on it.

The show, I am bound to say, merited an enthusiastic response. A cast of all the best Footlights guest artists did their stuff, topped off by Romaine Rand's fabled strip-tease nun routine, making its first appearance since the Sydney University revue several years before. For its reincarnation in the Pembroke smoker, she had hand-sewn a whole new Carmelite nun's habit. She wore a particularly daring bikini underneath. Luckily, the Dean didn't see the show until the last night, when he bit through the stem of his pipe.

Though Romaine pulled the walls in, really there was nothing in the show which did not go down a storm, mainly because the audience was clinically intoxicated, but partly because, in my role as producer, I had arranged the running order with some care, making sure that the up-beat songs came at the end of the half and stuff like that. I even got away with my own monologue. A whimsical little number about two railway locomotives in love, it went on for so long that the Hearties, from a sitting start, managed to reduce their table to matchwood before I was halfway through. But the show had built up too much impetus to be easily stopped. Since the whole of the university's theatrical establishment turned up over the course of the four nights, this small success could be counted as my first tangible impact on the broader Cambridge scene.

Clive James

Cambridge also has a Chancellor, Prince Philip, who may not be Cambridge-educated but who must have made almost more after-dinner speeches than any man alive. There are those who seem to think that HRH cannot open his mouth without putting his foot in it, but, speaking as his biographer, I have always thought HRH had a rather neat, if sometimes tart, turn of phrase. All his so-called 'gaffes' were off-the-cuff remarks, usually in what he imagined were private conversations. But that's not really the point, which is that, when called upon to do so, Prince Philip does after-dinner with the best of them. Here is an example.

To the French Chamber of Commerce

Je suis très honoré de votre invitation à dîner ce soir et de profiter de cette occasion de prendre la parole à la Chambre de Commerce Française à Londres.

Et merci aussi Monsieur le Président, pour m'avoir si bien reçu.

I apologise for not going on in French. I ought to be able to as I lived about eight years in St Cloud and went to school there. Even a wonderful State Visit, which I am certain all Paris enjoyed almost as much as we did, wasn't long enough to bring my French back to a reasonable standard. But both for your sakes and for mine I think it would be better and more understandable if I continue in English. French with an English accent has a certain limited use, and I think it was Lloyd George who said that the only person he could understand in French was Sir Edward Grey the Foreign Secretary. Statesmen are naturally in special danger and Sir Winston Churchill, who has his own brand of French and his own variety of wit, produced a classic.

The story, which shows signs of a fertile imagination, goes that Churchill appeared at Versailles wearing the cap and jacket of an Elder Brother of Trinity House. Clemenceau is supposed to have asked him about the strange outfit he was wearing, to which the reply was, 'Je suis un frère aîné de la Trinité.' This apparently was too much for Clemenceau, who is supposed to have said, 'Mon Dieu, quelle influence!'

Of course the stories about mistranslations are legion, and at one time there was almost a craze for phrases described as 'Fractured French' – I am sure you remember them: for instance, 'Pas de deux' became 'Father of twins'; 'Mal de mer' became 'Mother-in-law'; 'Mise en scène' – 'there are mice in the river'; and many other translations. 'Honi soit qui mal y pense' – 'honestly, I believe I'm going to be sick'; 'Chateau briand' – 'your hat is on fire'.

Naturally the fighting during the First World War produced a splendid crop of misunderstandings, like the pilot trying to explain what had happened to him: 'J'ai crashé dans les rognons,' which he fondly hoped to mean that he had crashed into a field of onions.

I'm always astonished by people who think that if they speak very loudly and slowly in their own language anyone abroad will understand them. I hope I'm not speaking too loud.

This is all very enjoyable but I dare say the members of this Chamber have advanced beyond these very elementary problems. For nearly eighty years it has been representing French commercial interests in this country with charm and success and I'm glad to hear with increasing activity.

There are two kinds of relations between states. There are the relations which exist between neighbours and there are the relations which exist between states which are not neighbours. The point about this is that only the two neighbours involved can begin to understand the relations which exist between them. Those married understand this is a strictly personal matter which others poke their noses into at their very grave peril. In current jargon it might be described as a love–hate relationship, irrational and unpredictable. It is in this context that the work of this Chamber must be judged, and from all I hear it manages to walk this tightrope with considerable success.

Prince Philip, Duke of Edinburgh

Prince Philip has always suffered at the hands of the press, most notably the Beaverbrook press. Lord Mountbatten and Beaverbrook struck up a firm feud based on who knows what. Mountbatten's sacrifice of the Beaver's fellow Canadians in the Dieppe Raid? Mountbatten's performance as last Viceroy of India? No one seems quite sure, though it gave Beaverbrook ample opportunity to indulge his insatiable love of mischief and malice. I missed Beaverbrook, joining his newspaper, the *Daily Express*, just over three years after his death. This, his last speech, is, I think, a real tour de force. It's almost more of a deathbed speech than a typical after-dinner number, and if the humour has a slightly dark edge it's none the worse for that. In a valedictory tribute in the *Sunday Express*, which he edited for so many years, John Gordon wrote,

Lord Beaverbrook's last speech

Shortly before the dinner Lord Beaverbrook was brought down to a room close to the dining-room. There he sat, resting. Lord Thomson came to lead him to the seat of honour.

'Let's go,' said Lord Beaverbrook, and rose from his chair.

Then an astonishing thing happened. For many weeks, he had been unable to move more than a few yards except in a wheelchair. A chair was waiting to take him into the dining-room. He never even looked at it.

Taking the arm of his son, Max, this amazing man walked slowly but steadily across the broad reception room and across the full length of the vast dining-room along the crowded tables. You could sense in his indomitable eyes, as he passed by, what the still dominant brain behind them was saying:

'This is the last time. I will walk to my place even if it kills me.'

To those who knew the condition he was in, those moving moments seemed an impossible miracle. An hour later he made that magnificent final speech of his life, so brilliant in content, so effective in delivery that it will be an unforgettable memory to all who heard it. Then, again on the arm of his proud son, he made the long walk back to the hotel entrance. There, he entered his car, and was driven twenty miles to his Surrey home where he went to bed, never to rise again.

John Gordon

I wish I'd been there but more than most it seems to me a speech which has a resonance and an echo even on the printed page so many years after the event.

Apprentice

My Lord Thomson of Fleet, Viscount Rothermere, my Lords and gentlemen: — I am deeply moved by the wonderful reception you have given me tonight. Also I am gratified for this present which I will esteem and value always.

It is quite true that I am old bones, my legs are very weak, but I still have something in the way of a head. I am still headstrong, and self-willed at that.

I will try to make you a speech tonight. But at eighty-five years of age, don't expect much. I cannot speak with the eloquence of Sir John Macdonald, born in Scotland, Canada's greatest orator and also Canada's greatest Prime Minister. He was my ideal. I hoped to follow his teaching. I heard him once. He was speaking from the platform of the last car of his private railway train. He fired me with enthusiasm for the British Empire. And I have been an Imperialist ever since. But not too successful, as you know.

In any case, in my eighty-sixth year, I must speak tonight. And it will be very easy indeed for me to make a better speech than Sir John could have delivered at the age of eighty-five. And I will tell you why. Because he died at seventy-six.

Many shrewd observers will say that I have not had any pattern, or continuous theme, in my long life. Certainly I have. But I have never been a successful leader. I have always been an apprentice, and never a master, and that has been a weakness in my political activities.

First I was an apprentice to finance in Canada. That was a life of daring adventure. In search of personal fortune and financial independence I promoted eleven companies. And may I say with humble gratitude that each of those eleven is a living example of leadership in commerce or industry in Canada at this very hour. But, of course, the leadership was not provided by me, but by those who came after me.

It was J. H. Thomas who said on the platform at the Albert Hall: 'When Max Aitken was a boy, he lived in a New Brunswick village with fifteen hundred other souls. It was too small for him, and he left for Halifax, a city of fifty thousand. It was too small for him, so he went to Montreal, where there are a quarter-of-a-million people. It was too small for him, so he left for London. He is here. One day London will be too small for him. And he will go to Hell. What then?' said Jim Thomas. 'I'll tell you – it won't be big enough for him.'

Well, I did go to London. And there I decided to become an apprentice in politics. After settling this grave issue about making a political career, I disposed of my Canadian business to my principal lieutenant, Killam. I took out my meagre share. And after fifty years Killam died worth a hundred and fifty millions. Perhaps I might have done more harm if I had stayed in Canada with all that money. However, I was by this time an apprentice to politics. And I sat six or seven years in the House of Commons, saying very little, but possibly learning a great deal.

War. And I served Lloyd George. It was a nerve-racking duty and it was hard to keep in step with that great Prime Minister. But I managed.

After war I became an apprentice in Fleet Street. And that was a real exciting experience.

At last, I thought, I will be a Master. Fancy free. Instead, I became the slave of the Black Art. I did not know freedom again for many a year.

I took over a bankrupt newspaper and lost plenty of money. I had dared to set up in rivalry to Northcliffe – the greatest journalist in the history of Fleet Street.

I was encouraged by the well-known lines:

He either fears his fate too much,
Or his deserts are small
That dares not put it to the touch
To gain or lose it all.

And I very nearly lost it all. Northcliffe had a Sunday paper. So I must have a Sunday paper, too. The *Sunday Express* added enormously to my losses. For several years I wondered: what will it be?

I began, of course, under the mistaken notion that I knew everything about the making of a good paper. Indeed, the curious and interesting thing about journalism is that everybody always knows far more about it than the journalist knows himself. You are subject to criticism – you receive some praise, I admit – but that praise is sometimes suspect. You are not entirely free from the influence of the sycophant – he is about you everywhere and always. But there is an extraordinary notion in the mind of mankind, a universal idea, that each and every one of us could run a newspaper, if we only had the chance, far better than the journalist could do it himself.

Well, I got the chance – I soon learned that I was a know-nothing. And after years of anxiety and much misery our papers began the slow but steady upward climb.

In learning about journalism I had to learn about journalists. Most of the guests here tonight are prominent in the vitally important and bitterly maligned profession of journalism.

No other profession is so heavily criticised. No other is preached at so much and told so often to mend its ways. Some of the loudest critics have a very simple code for us. It is this: 'Don't ever print anything about me that I wouldn't want people to read.'

I am not much impressed by all the talk about standards and codes. The code of a good journalist should be written within himself. It should not be written on parchment but

written on his heart. First, he must be true to himself. The man who is not true to himself is no journalist. He must show courage, independence and initiative. He must also, I believe, be a man of optimism. He has no business to be a peddler of gloom and despondency. He must be a respecter of persons, but able to deal with the highest and the lowest on the same basis, which is regard for the public interest and a determination to get at the facts.

The demands made on a journalist's character and sense of duty are heavy. Not every journalist meets the demands in full, but I am proud to say that in my long experience the vast majority of our journalists are an honour to their calling, and that the nation would be much poorer if these men, and women too, were not there to protect the nation from hidden scandals and secret misuse of power. I take more pride in my experience as a journalist than in any other experience I have had in a long and varied life.

149

Journalism and Politics are closely allied. My political faith was always strong, and many of you will say, also way-ward.

For many years I talked and wrote about the Empire. My campaign was welcomed with enthusiasm. Much support and triumphant results in the Constituencies were followed by indifference and finally rejection. Opponents would say: 'Well, if the Empire means so much to you, why don't you go back home again?'

My campaign dwindled. Public attention was focused on world panic and my plans were overwhelmed by failure and my movement was extinguished. Comfort there was none. I took refuge in reflecting on the fate of my Scottish hero James Graham, first Marquis of Montrose. His campaign failed. And you all know what happened to him. In the merry month of May in 1650, almost to this day, they hanged him in the Grass Market in Edinburgh.

I am not for a moment comparing myself with the great general and poet. Even on the contemporary scene I have been a minor figure, while Montrose's name will live for-ever. I am only comparing our fates. Both of us came to failure after initial success, and both of us were let down. Montrose was let down, strange to say, by the Earl of Home, and I was let down by the present Earl of Home's predecessor. You know who I mean. I am happy to say that the comparison stops there. Unlike Montrose, I was not let down at the end of a rope.

The Second World War, and once more an apprentice. This time to Industrial Production, under Churchill's guid-ance, and he sustained me. Without his support I would have failed completely in my task. I didn't stand a chance without his backing.

We were so ill-prepared. Our peril was beyond compre-hension. Churchill, after taking office, said to me: 'We will come through in triumph but we may lose our tail feathers.' In that belief in victory he remained steadfast through three years of incredible misfortunes. He never wavered, always steadily looking forward to the day of victory.

What was the genius of this great leader? Many have tried to analyse it. It was incomparable greatness in two spheres. There are men with a magnificent command of words but with a very poor command of events. There are formidable men of action who lack the gift of inspiration. With Churchill, the thought, the word and the deed were one. His war speeches were like Nelson's signal at Trafalgar. They were action in themselves. Confident, defiant and immortal, they strengthened the heart and the hand of all engaged in the deadly struggle. Churchill's speeches mobilised the best that was in us.

Until I became Minister of Aircraft Production in Churchill's government, I had always associated 'bottlenecks' with pleasure. But the Aircraft Ministry was the biggest bottleneck that was ever known.

The air frames could be produced. But where was the harness? A bottleneck. Where were the power plants? Another bottleneck. And the guns – ·303 and 20 mm? None of it: the air frames were but skeletons.

The very word 'bottleneck' meant gloom and misery to me.

But the bottlenecks were overcome and also the enemy.

What about the new world?

What about the prophecies of what the world would be like after the war?

The greatest foresight was that of a murderer – a man condemned to die. He escaped because he was crazy. His name was Hess, Deputy Chancellor of Germany. He came to Scotland in 1941, on a one-way journey.

I was sent by Churchill to interview him. And I tried to make out just why he came. Was he in flight from Germany? Was he a refugee? He said not. He came to negotiate peace with Britain on any terms providing Britain would join Germany in attacking our ally, Russia.

'A victory for England', he said, 'will be a victory for the Bolsheviks. A Bolshevik victory will sooner or later mean Russian occupation of Germany and the rest of Europe. England would be as incapable of hindering it as any other nation.'

Shortly after Hess made these remarkable predictions, I left under the direction of Churchill for Russia to make a treaty – not for peace, but war.

In Moscow, Stalin said to me: 'Britain means to make peace with Germany, leaving Russia to fight alone.'

I asked him: 'What makes you think that?'

'Hess is your line of communication with Hitler,' he said.

'Oh, no,' I said.

'Why then do you not shoot him?'

'He must be tried,' I answered.

'Why did he come to Britain?'

That was the question I was waiting for. I produced the transcript of my conversation with Hess, and also a memo he sent me in his own hand, proposing that Britain should make peace with Germany on our terms providing we would join in a German–British attack on Russia. I told him that Churchill had rejected the plan with contempt.

A word of advice to our friend Lord Thomson of Fleet. He praised my achievements in journalism. Well, I am going to praise his triumphs in television.

What a fine title – Lord Thomson of Fleet! How did Northcliffe and Rothermere, Riddell and Lord Dalziel, and I and some others give him an opportunity of taking that title? I cannot make out. We could have been in before him. But I have a piece of advice to give him, from the very depths of my heart. It is this. That he should be guided by my wisdom and gain benefit by my experience. He should begin a new career at once – become an apprentice as quickly as possible. Give up these newspapers of his and take to politics, or philanthropy, or something or other, so long as he ceases to trouble our little group of newspaper proprietors.

We were so agreeably placed until he came along to disturb the waters of tranquillity.

Here I must say, in my eighty-sixth year, I do not feel greatly different from when I was eighty-five. This is my final word. It is time for me to become an apprentice once more. I have not settled in which direction. But somewhere, sometime soon.

Lord Beaverbrook

Which brings me, ladies and gentlemen, to Mr Gyles Brandreth. Something was always going to bring me to Mr Brandreth in a book of this nature, for Mr Brandreth in the late twentieth and earliest years of the twenty-first century spoke after dinner for Britain. No meal in those years could be a real dinner without the toastmaster banging his gavel and shouting out, 'My Lords, ladies and gentlemen, pray silence for Mr Gyles Brandreth.'

What first brought me to Mr Brandreth was the *Daily Express*, which sent me to his rooms in New College, Oxford in the late 1960s. Mr Brandreth was the Beverley Nichols of his day. There seemed nothing of which he was not the president or the editor, and he was already famous for the felicity of his spoken word. In the ensuing years he won a reputation for wearing extravagant pullovers on television, for teddy bears and, yes, for after-dinner speaking. He was in the *Guinness Book of Records* for it.

Then, in 1992, Mr Brandreth was elected as Member of Parliament for the city of Chester, and in the same year he was invited to present a Ten Minute Rule bill. This is not the same as being asked to deliver an after-dinner speech but Mr Brandreth pretended it was. The former Conservative MP, Matthew Parris, was in the chamber reporting for *The Times*. This is what he wrote:

Matthew Parris

On Gyles Brandreth

Gyles Brandreth has decided to do within Parliament what he does best outside it. Mr Brandreth speaks after dinner. He believes in free speech but not free speeches. For decades he has been making rather good ones, for money. As dusk fell yesterday, the House enjoyed a rare treat: a top-class after-dinner Brandreth speech – but before dinner, and free. His subject was his proposed new bill (it will never become law) to encourage the use of 'plain language' in consumer contracts . . . If we were to judge his perform-ance yesterday, we could do no better than quote Sir Noël Coward's impromptu response upon unexpectedly meeting the schmaltzy American pianist, Liberace, on the *Queen Mary*. 'How do you do, Mr Liberace.' (Embarrassed pause) 'I think you do' (pause) 'what you do' (pause) 'very well.'

Gobbledegook or small print

Madam Speaker.

I beg to move,

That leave be given to bring in a Bill to secure improvements to the language and layout of certain contracts.

Language is what distinguishes the human race; it is the characteristic that sets us apart and makes us unique. Even I, as an ardent animal lover, must acknowledge that, however eloquently a dog may bark, he cannot tell us that his parents were poor but honest. Language makes us unique, and we in this country are born with the privilege of having a unique language as our parent tongue – English, the richest language in the history of humanity.

Our language is rich precisely because it is not pure. Emerson called it 'the sea which receives tributaries from every region under heaven'. It is the language of Chaucer and the King James Bible; of Keats, Joyce, Anthony Trollope and Anthony Burgess. It has taken 2,000 years to reach this far – and where is it now, in 1992? Let me show you, Madam Speaker, by quoting from the terms of sale offered by that excellent builders' merchant, Jewson Ltd:

If and to the extent that any person by whom the Seller has been supplied with the goods supplied hereunder (hereinafter referred to as "the Supplier") validly excludes restricts or limits his liability to the Seller in respect of the said goods or of any loss or damage arising in connection therewith the liability of the Seller to the Buyer in respect of the said goods or of any loss or damage arising in connection therewith shall be correspondingly excluded restricted or limited.

There you have it, Madam Speaker: the English language today – and those were just five of more than 100 such lines that feature on the back of the Jewson delivery note. When the driver drops off the breeze block and says, 'Sign here,

guy,' what I have just read out constitutes 5 per cent. of what the recipient is agreeing to – whether he likes it or not, and whether he understands it or not.

Does it matter? Yes, I believe that it does. It cannot be good that people regularly sign contracts that they do not understand, and, indeed, are not meant to understand.

[Mr Dennis Skinner (Bolsover): Has the hon. Gentleman read the Maastricht treaty?]

As it happens, I have and I understood it, but I can understand that it might be a little sophisticated for the hon. Gentleman. However, the rest of this is in plain English, so he will feel wholly at home.

Costly mistakes can be made. A constituent of mine discovered that when he signed an incomprehensible contract to lease a photocopier. When he wanted to change the photocopier, he was faced with the option of a so-called settlement charge of about £10,000, which was three times the value of the original equipment, or the prospect of leasing the equipment, whose lifetime according to the manufacturer was three years, for a total of seven years. None of that was clear from the contract whose wording was deliberately obfuscatory and arcane.

The Bill is designed to encourage the use of clear, plain language in commercial contracts and to prevent the unscrupulous, arrogant or incompetent from hiding behind legalese, jargon, gobbledegook or small print. It would apply to consumer contracts, consumer credit contracts – think of all the confusion that we would all be spared if we understood the small print that comes with our Access cards – and housing contracts . . .

A plain language law might appear to be a contradiction in terms because is it not the law and lawyers which are responsible for much of the gobbledegook found in contracts? I believe I am right in saying that in 1595 an English Chancellor chose to make an example of a particularly wordy document filed in his court. He ordered a hole to be cut in the centre of the document – all 120 pages of it – and had the author's head stuffed through it. The offender was then led around Westminster hall, 100 yards from where we are now – even 100 metres – as an example to all and sundry. Alas, that Elizabethan lesson did not stick; and that is where I come in, four centuries later but not a moment too soon.

I propose that the contracts covered by the Bill should be written in clear and readily understandable language using words with common and everyday meanings, be arranged in a logical order, be suitably divided into paragraphs and headings, be clearly laid out and be easily legible . . .

The case for such a law is overwhelming. Clear, coherent, easy-to-read consumer contracts bring advantages to consumers and to business, but the signs of voluntary implementation are piecemeal. I believe that, as in the United

States, the chief merit of the new law would be its impetus for change. Alas, only legislation will prompt businesses to sit up and start to take notice of their own paperwork.

I trust that the advantages of the Bill will be obvious to the House. Inevitably, some people will not see its virtues, but then, as the saying has it, a slight inclination of the cranium is as adequate as a spasmodic movement of one optic to an equine quadruped utterly devoid of visionary capacity.

Gyles Brandreth

Three years later, in 1995, Gyles Brandreth was invited to second the Loyal Address on the occasion of the Queen's opening of Parliament. He was able to confirm that the Queen's Speech in the Queen's English was exactly *comme il faut* – unlike the occasion on which he was asked to unveil a plaque in his constituency. He had pulled the little string and the blue velvet curtains parted to reveal the words:

This plaque has been unveiled by Gyles Brandreth MP.

Well, as Will Rogers once said: 'I tell you Folk, all Politics is Apple Sauce.' You would have thought that was the attitude of a collection of very bright young things brought together in the 1970s under the presiding genius of Lord (Victor) Rothschild – a brilliant scion of the banking family who also once opened the batting for Harrow against Eton at Lord's with the playwright Terence Rattigan – surely one of the most improbable opening partnerships in the history of cricket. Convened to advise on government strategy, their official title was the CPRS (Central Policy Review Staff) but they were popularly known as the 'Think Tank'. The Think Tank dined every year at the Mirabelle Restaurant in London, and instead of formal speeches they read out spoof telegrams purporting to have been written by the great and the good of the day. Like many of the best after-dinnerisms they were specific to the occasion and to those present: the epitome of the 'in-joke'. This therefore is part of a story which is, perhaps, only perfectly comprehended by those present. However, every mock-telegram tells a story, and for students of twentieth-century politics each one is a small nugget of historical footnote.

Top secret

APPEARANCE OF CENTRAL POLICY REVIEW STAFF AT CHEQUERS LAST WEEK WAS UNIQUE OCCASION IN ANNALS OF BRITISH CABINET. LONG MAY IT REMAIN SO! BURKE TREND*

KEEP UP GOOD WORK OF POURING WATER ON TROUBLED OILS. BARRAN†

CHAIRMAN ROTHSCHILD SINK TANK. FROM ONE WHO HAS THOUGHTS TO ANOTHER. GLEETINGS MAO

MANY THANKS FOR YOUR STRATEGY PAPER. PUBLISHING TOMORROW. CHAPMAN PINCHER‡

MIRABELLE JUNKETINGS PREMATURE. SUGGEST IMMEDIATE RETURN TO DRAWING BOARD. E. HEATH

HAVE NOTED WITH INTEREST PROMINENT ROLE OF CENTRAL POLICY REVIEW STAFF IN DEVELOPMENT OF TORY STRATEGY. YOUR MEMBERS MAY REST ASSURED THAT THIS WILL NOT BE FORGOTTEN WHEN I COME TO FORM MY ALTERNATIVE ADMINISTRATION. H. WILSON

The fact is that the best after-dinner stories belong to an occasion. The sprightly Miles Kington, an old *Punch* hand, who for years has contributed an enviably inventive humorous column to the *Independent*, reminds us of the dangers of forgetting this.

---

* Sir Burke Trend, GCB, CVO (now the Right Hon. Lord Trend), then Secretary of the Cabinet.
† Sir David Barran, at that time Chief Executive of the Royal Dutch Shell Group and therefore Lord Rothschild's former employer.
‡ The famous *Daily Express* journalist.

Ten ways NOT to start a funny story

'If you have ever heard me speak before, you will know that one of my favourite stories is the one about . . .'

'Well, if you didn't think that one was funny I just know you'll like this one . . .'

'You probably know this one, but I'll tell it anyway . . .'

'This one's a really funny story . . .'

'Stop me if you've heard it . . .'

'So anyway . . .'

'So anyway, there was this . . .'

'There was this Jew and this Arab and they were in a bar together – no, hang on a moment it wasn't a bar because Arabs don't drink, so let's say it was a train, yes, it was a train, and there was this Arab came in and said to the Jew – no hold on I think it was a bar . . .'

'Did I ever tell you the one where the man is playing golf and his wife's funeral procession goes by? No, hold on, I've just told you the punchline . . .'

'I can't remember the punchline at the moment, but I'm sure it'll come back to me as I tell the story . . .'

Miles Kington

My learned friend John Mortimer tells some of the best after-dinner stories around, and does so in that dry, sardonic lawyer's manner which is peculiarly English and which I find particularly enjoyable. It's a slightly unfashionable mode of address these days, sometimes being thought old-fashioned and upper class. For me both characteristics enhance the enjoyment. This oration was made after a Folio Society dinner and was allegedly part of a debate. The subject was 'These days crime fiction is more interesting than the real thing', and P. D. James spoke for the motion in persuasive fashion. But Sir John was able to steal the show (and the vote) by gently tweaking some of his best stories to fit his case for the opposition. To be taken, I think, ladies and gentlemen, with a vintage port, a decent Havana and a dry chuckle. Not to mention a pinch of salt.

Stranger than fiction

Ladies and gentlemen: first I must ascertain, can you all hear me? Well, that's a great pity – because I was about to tell you my Rumpole audibility joke. There's Rumpole sitting next to the prosecutor and this terrible little judge comes bobbing into court, and Rumpole turns to the prosecutor and says, 'I don't know whether you've got any experience of this judge, but he's an absolute four-letter man, he's an absolute pain in the bottom. He is pompous, boring, tedious, unfair, deaf, unjust, the most unappealing little judge you could ever have appeared before.' And the judge says, 'Mr Rumpole, it may surprise you to know that the acoustics in this court are absolutely perfect, and I can hear every single word that is uttered on counsel's benches.' And Rumpole turns to the prosecutor and says, 'See what I mean?'

I'm not in the least surprised that Baroness James, one of the most perfect performers in the art of crime fiction, should come here and support fiction as opposed to real life. Phyllis James is perhaps the lady whom I admire most in our civilisation. She is not only a masterly writer, but also a wonderful woman who, in every sphere of life – the BBC, the Arts Council, the House of Lords, that very arcane institution, the Royal Society of Literature, where we sit together drinking tea and eating fruit-cake once a month – is a master, a mistress, of the common-sense approach; and if the running of our society and the running of our country were left to Phyllis James, we should have absolutely nothing to worry about. It doesn't surprise me that being a mistress of common sense, and sterling good sense, she is opposed to the total fantasy, the strange art, the weird convolutions of reality, and dedicated to the mundane, strong, common sense of fiction.

I can perhaps speak from both sides of the coin, because I have sat, and sometimes slept, through cases in the Old Bailey, and have taken part in that weird world in which old gentlemen dress up in wigs and dressing-gowns and every-body is pretending to be someone else: judges are acting judges and saying, 'What is a tee-shirt?'; barristers are acting humility and saying, 'If your lordship pleases, with very great respect,' to someone for whom they lost all respect many years ago; criminals are touching their forelocks and pretending to be cheerful, cockney characters and saying, 'Thank you, my lord, fourteen years, that'll do me very nicely.' I have gone down from the Old Bailey to the rehearsal room and sat among a company of actors trying to behave with common sense and tell the truth about the world in some work of fiction. But looking back on it, the 'real' world is really the most interesting because it is the most extraordinary and the most unexpected, and it far surpasses fiction in these qualities. The art of writing a Rumpole story has forever been to try to *tame* reality, to get it to fit into a work of fiction which someone will believe, because if you put it down neat and took it unadulterated, no one would credit it.

Talking about violent death, may I just read you a bit of reality. This is a quotation from the Edinburgh *Evening News* of 18 August 1978 – perhaps that's even 'today':

While they were waiting at a bus stop in Cleriston, Mr and Mrs Daniel Thirsty were threatened by a Mr Robert Clear. 'He demanded that I gave him my wife's purse,' said Mr Thirsty. 'Telling him that the purse was in her basket, I bent down, put my hands up her skirt, detached her artificial leg and hit him over the head with it. It was not my intention to do more than frighten him off, but, unhappily for us, he died.'

Well, put that in a Rumpole or even somewhere in a work by Phyllis James or Ruth Rendell – those great geniuses that sit here tonight – and the audience might look a little askance.

I took to crime somewhat late in life – it's an interesting occupation and it does pay, particularly if you do it on the legal aid. But before then I'd done nothing other than divorce and will cases; and, as clients, I found murderers greatly preferable to those in will cases and divorce cases. They had rather higher moral standards than clients in divorce cases, and they behaved rather better than families quarrelling over the possession of their aunty's toast rack. *And* they had the great advantage of being under lock and key so they couldn't ring you up in the middle of the night. But, of course, Phyllis James is absolutely right – murder, like Christmas, goes on in the family circle. It goes on between husband and wife, between lovers, between land-lords and tenants, between friends. But that doesn't, surely, make it any less interesting – those are the great dramatic moments of our lives . . .

One thing about murderers is that, as clients, they are usually very peaceful people because they've killed the one person in life whom they really needed to get rid of, and a kind of quiescence of the soul enters upon them. The other thing that you don't really get in fiction is the extraordinary reaction of judges to murders, particularly when they are judges who have spent most of their lives doing planning applications and have never seen blood in any shape or form. I remember defending a dwarf – this again was a landlord-and-tenant murder – and the dwarf had murdered his landlord, who was an extremely tall Irishman. In order to commit this act, the dwarf had to stand on a soap-box and strike his landlord on the head with a length of lead piping. I defended this dwarf – I have to say unsuccessfully – to the best of my ability, and the judge, in passing judgment, looked at the dwarf and said, 'You, dwarf, are a mixture between Clytemnestra and Lady Macbeth.' Well, I don't think the dwarf particularly objected to going to prison for life, but to be called a mixture between Clytemnestra and Lady Macbeth was really going a bit too far. I don't know in how many works of fiction a judgment starts, 'You, dwarf, are a mixture between Clytemnestra and Lady Macbeth.' . . .

And then, again, the actual process of murder cases is something that is very difficult for the person who just sits and writes fiction to experience. I remember the panoply, the extraordinary pageantry, that went on at the Old Bailey, and I remember defending a gentleman who was meant to have murdered someone in a 'tuberculosis' van (one of those vans where you go to get your lungs checked). He was brought up from the cells on the opening day of the Old Bailey; he was brought up from the darkness into the light of the court and there, on the bench, the first thing he saw was a sheriff with a fur muff on his head, carrying a huge sword, rapidly followed by the Lord Mayor of London wearing a black cocked hat with ostrich feathers, rapidly followed by a judge in scarlet and ermine sniffing a nosegay. And my unfortunate client shouted out, 'The Day of Judgment is at hand,' and had to be removed to Broadwell Asylum for the insane.

I remember when a bomb was thrown outside the Old Bailey while I was defending a young man for the attempted murder of a policeman. He'd filled his car with petrol, hadn't paid for it, and had driven off; so a policeman tried to stop the car and was impaled on the bonnet. The policeman survived, but the young man was charged with attempted murder. The case wasn't going too well when suddenly the judge, a very slow and pompous judge, got a note, very slowly opened it, and said: 'Members of the jury, we have got a note here, and, members of the jury, I will read this note, if the members of the jury will allow – THERE'S A BOMB OUTSIDE THE BUILDING!' And he shot, like a rabbit out of a trap, into Ludgate Circus, and we all assembled there while the judge read his books to try and discover where you take the verdict from a jury in Ludgate Circus. He decided we couldn't, the jury went back, and the young man was acquitted.

I haven't been in a court for ten years, so I'm not really qualified to talk about this motion that is all about 'today'. But the other day I got a taxi, and the taxi driver asked if I still did those cases down at the Old Bailey. I said, 'No, I haven't been there for nine or ten years.' And he said, 'I was on the jury the day the bomb went off outside the Old Bailey.' 'Well, you were a very nice jury,' I said, 'because you acquitted my young man of the attempted murder of the policeman.' He said, 'Oh, yes, we did. Well, every morning, when you came into the court, you said good-morning to us and the prosecutor *never* said good-morning.' So maybe it isn't all down to the eloquence of Sir Norman Birkin.

But there it is. Of course *Othello* is marvellous, of course Phyllis James is marvellous, of course Ruth Rendell is superbly marvellous: of course all these writers are marvellous. But where *Othello* comes from, jealousy hasn't died, envy hasn't died, family feuds and hatred haven't died, and where you find them first of all is sitting in cells with people who look strangely ordinary and who tell you things that are absolutely astonishing. And life doesn't change, crime doesn't change, evil is still there and still inexplicable. It has to be translated, it has to be made understandable, it has, strangely enough, in fiction to have order and credibility implanted on it. And, in fact, order and credibility are what, in reality, it frequently doesn't have.

I'd like briefly to end with another factual case which happened in a place called Southsea: it is about a very unsuccessful attempt to murder a spouse. Dwarfing all known records for matrimonial homicide, Mr Peter Scott made seven attempts to kill his wife, without her once noticing that anything was wrong. In 1980 he took out an insurance policy on his good lady which would bring him £250,000 in the event of her accidental death. Soon afterward, he placed a lethal dose of mercury in her strawberry flan, but it all rolled out. Not wishing to waste the lethal substance, he then stuffed her mackerel with the entire contents of the bottle. This time she ate it, with no side effects whatsoever. Warming to the task, he took his wife on holiday to Yugoslavia. Recommending the panoramic views, he invited her to sit on the edge of a cliff – she declined to do so, prompted by what she later described as 'some sort of sixth sense'. The same occurred only weeks later when he asked her to savour the view from Beachy Head. While his spouse was in bed

with chicken-pox he started a fire outside the bedroom door, but some interfering busybody put it out. Undeterred, he started another fire and burnt down the whole flat in Turswell Road, Southsea: the wife of his bosom escaped uninjured. Another time he asked her to stand in the middle of the road so that he could drive towards her and check if his brakes were working. At no time did Mrs Scott feel that the magic had gone out of their marriage. Since it appeared that nothing short of a small nuclear bomb would have alerted this good woman to her husband's intentions, he eventually gave up and confessed all to the police. After the case, a detective said that Mrs Scott was absolutely shattered when told of her husband's plot to kill her. She had not clued it at all and she was dumbstruck.

The truth, members of the jury, the truth, the whole truth, nothing but the truth: nothing whatever to do with fiction. I hope you all vote for us – for me.

John Mortimer

The Trollope Society has a kinship with The Folio Society and annually it dines. After one such dinner, the novelist Joanna Trollope was invited to speak. She is not directly descended from the great Anthony, but, as William Rees-Mogg said in his introduction, 'She has really, in an extraordinary way, followed her eminent quasi-forebear, in that she combines what he enormously valued – which is a very high degree of readability, a genuine popularity – with an acuteness and sharpness of insight which makes a popular novel almost indubitably a serious one.'

Her subject on this particular evening, and without, as she said, any beating about coy bushes, was Trollope and sex:

Trollope and sex

My trusty Chambers dictionary – which I infinitely prefer to its Oxford equivalent – says, among other definitions, that sex is the quality of being male or female. This essential truth is one that Trollope understood perfectly. He understood the differences in the way men and women think, and feel, but he also understood, most tellingly, the way that most men and women make little dashes every so often into each other's traditionally held territories. So that when Lady Glencora has a few bravura skirmishes among the high pinnacles of politics, and Johnny Eames (who I fear makes me impatient) makes it plain that his love for Lily Dale is his whole world and not for him a thing apart, Trollope uses both merely to emphasise the femaleness of the former and the maleness of the latter.

With this outstanding grasp upon the intrinsic business of gender, it isn't surprising that Trollope turned out to be brilliant at writing about sex. He is even, dare I say it, the best at it among the Victorians.

Dickens, let's face it, is pretty hopeless in this respect. True love, in his novels, comes too often in simpering, infantile form – the notion of taking Dora Copperfield to bed is positively indecent – or wrapped up respectably in the wings of the Angel in the Home. If any kind of sexual allure does begin to pace enticingly in the shadows – Estella in *Great Expectations*, for example – you know it will be sentimentalised into the reformed (and therefore no longer dangerously sexy) good woman by the end.

George Eliot even, not a novelist to baulk at any taboo, is also a little odd about sex. Her men are allowed to hear its siren call – why else for example, should Dr Lydgate have married so disastrously? – but the women are not. They can be very passionate and very frustrated, but George Eliot wants them to channel all this emotional vehemence into intellectual life. And Thackeray – dear Thackeray – knew, one feels, a good deal about sex and its complications, but something held him back in his heart when writing; even in *Vanity Fair*, where Becky Sharp, even though she uses sexual wiles with pure calculation, is in essence a cold fish, and Thackeray knows it. One of the great subtleties of the portrayal of Becky Sharp is that she knew all about sex – but she couldn't feel it.

What separates Trollope from his contemporaries was that he did, as a writer, feel about sex, and powerfully at that. Despite the fact that nineteenth-century conventions demanded that much of what he wrote about sex was either implied or coded, he nonetheless makes absolutely plain both the sexual nature of his characters and their response to it, women as well as men.

It is fascinating to look at his women in this light because he was so very frank about the aura that sensual experience – either past or present or, for an engaged girl, enticingly in the future – gave them. There is no doubt of the almost electric radiance that Lady Glencora gives off when that dangerous, rapturous waltz with Burgo Fitzgerald confirms her both as being in love and having a heady dose of violent physical attraction. Madame Max Goesler, almost at times a caricature of the mystery beauty from Mittel Europe, is plainly sexually experienced: it is part of her sophistication, though she carries her knowledge about with her with the utmost discretion. She has to do this to keep her place in society, and Trollope makes no bones about his anger at women's attitudes to one another over sex. He deplores the intolerance women display to one another, even writing with some heat in *An Eye For An Eye*, that if a woman over-steps the mark in the opinion of the sisterhood, 'then a woman ceases to be a woman in the eyes of her own sex'.

Perhaps that is why Lily Dale took the line she did. I can't share the Prime Minister's [John Major's] enthusiasm for her, but I am much intrigued by the suggestion made by a reader of Exeter University that Lily was not in fact a virgin, that she had slept with Crosbie, and that that accounted for her adamant insistence thereafter that she was, in all truth, his wife. She needed to believe it in order not to feel she had disgraced herself, her self-esteem, and her gender, and in order to avoid having the fatal finger pointed at her. Yet if Lady Laura Kennedy never slept with Phineas Finn, she would have sold her soul to do so. She is one of the most subtle and poignant of all Trollope's portraits of women, a plain, clever, rich aristocratic woman who uses her power mistakenly in matters of the heart, and is then punished by an obsessive, passionate longing for a man she might once have had. And she, consumed by this longing and subverting all her ideals and principles helplessly to it, hardly cares who knows.

These women, of course, with the exception of Lily Dale, have money. Trollope, realist as he was, was under no illusion as to the sexual charm of wealth. Riches, and sometimes a title too, lend a lusciousness to the otherwise not entirely enticing persons of Miss Dunstable, the fearful de Courcy girls, even grubby little Lizzie Eustace. They give Madame Max a power in addition to her experience and her exotic olive-skinned looks, a wonderful power to which even the supremely selfish old Duke of Omnium is susceptible and which he tries to augment by leaving her all his jewels.

Yet even some of Trollope's poorer girls have, if not sexual power, then healthy sexual appetites, which they display in their spirited, often challenging, attitudes to their more privileged lovers. 'I adore you,' they seem to say, 'but I'm quite as good as you. And I can prove it.' Girls like Mary Thorne and Lucy Robarts and Ayala Dormer are almost Trollope's pets. He knows how much they have to lose; he knows that this courtship and marriage business is of such alarming and consummate importance to them that whatever physical enthusiasm they feel for Frank Gresham and Lord Lufton they must sternly repress it lest it catches the eye of a deeply disapproving potential mother-in-law.

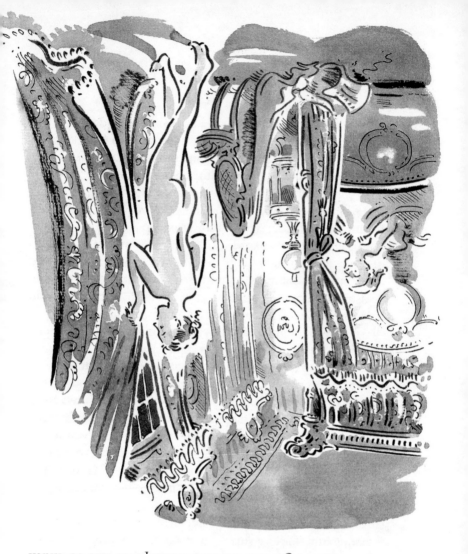

Only sometimes does Trollope resign himself to the fact that some good sweet girls simply have no sex appeal at all. Poor dreary little Grace Crawley is such a one, and I'm afraid I have my doubts too about Eleanor Harding. Her elder sister, on the other hand, is another matter. I have a strong suspicion that some robustly pleasant times were had behind the drawn bed curtains in the rectory at Plumstead Episcopi. That is, if Susan Grantly could ever get the Archdeacon to shut up.

Which brings me to Trollope men. Now here we are on more delicate ground because Trollope is not so much observing and understanding and loving as he is with women, but knowing. Naturally he knew, first and foremost, about himself. He makes it perfectly plain in his *Autobiography* that he detested his appearance and believed himself to be extremely unattractive. He also hints, during those dingy early years as a Post Office clerk, in what he called his 'hobbledehoyhood', at the seedy sexual encounters of any unsupervised young man at large in Victorian London without much money. Yet as he grew older, he grew bolder. Dogged always by his own weird mixture of bombast and shyness, he nevertheless was unafraid of women. Indeed he loved them, all his life, from his frequently unlovable mother onwards. He describes the society of women as giving 'comfort and excitement'; he writes lingeringly of their looks, of their particular glamour on horseback, of their challenge and wit and sweetness and imperiousness. His pages seem to light up when women enter, and a relish seems to infuse his prose. No wonder, being what he was and wondering what he did, that he felt so about sex.

Yet, curiously, his approach to sexuality in men is less confident than it is in women; at times it is almost opaque. There is the unavoidable fact that his heroes, his 'white hats', whom he will finally award to his beloved girls, have little or no sex appeal. That procession of beautiful young men – and how he emphasises their beauty, almost as if in painful contrast to his own lack of it – like Lord Lufton and Henry Crawley and Phineas Finn, are to the modern eye tremendously unfanciable. Can it be simply a change of fashion in what we find attractive that those tall, light-eyed, bearded public school boys of Trollope's have all the contemporary sex appeal of pillars of salt? Odd if so, since Trollope's women have retained every particle of their charms. But the boys appear insipid now, and frequently childishly self-absorbed, even Phineas Finn, in whose Irishness I can never quite believe. There is only one among their number who has what it takes that I can think of, and that is Colonel

Jonathan Stubbs in *Ayala's Angel*. And he is very interesting, not so much for what he is, as for what he reveals about Trollope. Because Colonel Stubbs, who is brave and funny and cool and slightly masterful and undeniably sexy, is also undeniably ugly. Trollope goes on and on about how ugly he is, with his red hair and bristling beard and his great wide mouth. Of course he has done wonderful soldierly things and sits a horse like a dream and has a lovely speaking voice and dances divinely but heavens, he's so ugly, Trollope says. But he also says that Ayala is excited by him. 'If only', she says to him before their marriage and plainly fearful that husbandhood will dim his physical glory for her, 'you could have been only my lover for a little longer?' So now we know.

It's the ugly ones that have it.

And also, interestingly, the bad ones: Trollope's 'black hats'. If few modern women in search of an adventure would accept a Frank Gresham, they would certainly consider Burgo Fitzgerald a possibility, and even Melmotte. Trollope's Jews are fascinating and definitely sexy, and that is the reason (and the subsequent reason for her shame) that such a one as Emily Wharton should marry another as Ferdinand Lopez. Trollope's Jews may have none of the blond, safe, sporting qualities he seems to expect us to admire in his heroes, but they have something much more compelling. They are comfortably in touch with their own sensuality, their own appetites, they are urban and exotic, in contrast to the red-faced fox-hunting men – even the repellent Reverend Emilius – and the women see it and respond to it. Trollope may not like it, it may threaten an Anglo-Saxon Protestant reticence in sexual matters even in him, but he is too honest to pretend it doesn't happen.

He is also too honest not to allow sex to make a fool of some men. The punishment of Obadiah Slope is not in worldly ways but far more realistically and subtly, in sexual ones. He becomes the sweating amorous plaything of Madeline Neroni, who has ingeniously incorporated being crippled into part of her sexual armoury, and then he stumbles about after Eleanor Bold at Miss Thorne's party, drunken and insistent, a great red ox confused by sexual frustration into public humiliation. It is an exquisite comeuppance.

It is also true. However delicately put, however much his characters are concealing from themselves or one another, there is truth in Trollope's observation about sex and truth in its portrayal. His people are as varied, as overt and as covert, as we are ourselves. If Anthony Trollope had lived long enough to hear the theories and discoveries of Sigmund Freud, I don't think he'd have heard much to surprise him.

Joanna Trollope

Robertson Davies, the distinguished Canadian novelist with the equally distinguished Trollopian beard, was also a friend of The Folio Society. When he spoke after dinner he really did tell a story. As Master of Massey College, the University of Toronto's equivalent of All Souls, Davies enlivened the annual Christmas feast by dazzling his fellow Fellows and their guests with a ghost story of his own concoction. 'It was never my intention to frighten anyone,' he said. 'Indeed, I do not think that would have been possible; the audience was too big and to me, at least, terror is best when the group of listeners is small. No, these stories were to amuse . . .' Don't believe a word of it. Lower the lights, ladies and gentlemen, sit back from your tables, hearken to the howl of the wind outside and the creak of the timber on the empty staircase. This is the Master of Massey at his best.

Refuge of insulted saints

'I see you have guests,' said the youngest of the Fellows, when we met last week at High Table. As he said it I thought he winked.

I made no answer, but I was conscious of turning pale.

'I noticed them in your guest-room a couple of times last week when I was at breakfast,' he persisted.

Of course he would have noticed them. He is an almost professionally observant young man. When he goes back to New Zealand I hope he puts his gift at the disposal of the Secret Service.

The design of this College is such that when the Fellows are taking their leisurely breakfast in the private dining-room they can look directly into the windows of my guest-chamber. Guests have often complained about it. Two or three ladies have used a disagreeable term: ogling. But the guests who are there now I had hoped – trusting, unworldly creature that I am – to keep from the eyes of the College, and if they have been seen it must be taken as evidence that whatever influence I once had over them is now dispelled. I long ago accepted the fact that this College is haunted, but until recently it has been my determination to keep appari-tions out of my own Lodging. But I know now that I have been cruelly betrayed by what, in justice to myself, I must call all the nobility and overflowing compassion of my own nature.

It all began this autumn, on the thirty-first of October. To be more accurate, it was a few minutes after midnight, and was therefore the first of November. The date and time are important, for of course the Eve of All Hallows, when evil spirits roam the earth, extends only until midnight, after which it is succeeded by All Hallows itself – All Saints' Day, in fact. I was lying in bed reading an appropriate book – the *Bardo Thodol.* For those of you whose Tibetan may have grown rusty I should explain that it is the great *Tibetan Book of the Dead*, a kind of guide book to the adventures of the spirit after it leaves this world. I had just reached the description of the Chonyid State, which is full of blood-drinking, brain-pulping and bone-gnawing by the Lord of Death, and as I read, I munched an apple. Then I became aware of a rattling at the College gate.

This happens often when the Porter has gone off duty and I have retired for the night. I frequently vow that never again will I get up and put on a dressing-gown and slippers and traipse out into the cold to see who it is. But I always do so. It is the compassion I have already spoken of as amounting almost to a weakness in my character that makes me do it. The rattler is often some girl who assures me that she simply must get back a paper that is being marked by one of the Teaching Fellows in the College. Or it may be that some young man has ordered a pizza and is too utterly fatigued by his studies to go down to the gate and get it for himself. It would be heartless to disregard such pathetic evidences of what it is now fashionable to call the Human Condition. So up I got and down I traipsed.

The night was cold and wet and dark, and as I peered through the gate – for of course I was on the inside – I could just make out the form of a girl, who seemed to have a bicycle with her.

'Make haste to open gate,' she said in a peremptory voice and with a marked foreign accent. 'I vant to see priest at vonce.'

'If you want a priest, young woman, you had better try Trinity,' said I.

'Phui for Trinity,' she snapped, insofar as an expression like 'Phui' may be snapped. 'Is here the Massey College, no? I vant Massey College priest. Be very quick, please.'

I was a prey to conflicting emotions. Who was this unde- niably handsome, rudely demanding girl? And whom could she mean by the Massey College priest? Our Chaplain lives out. Could it be our Hall Don? A priest undoubtedly but – was he leading a double life? Or was this girl a bait to lure him forth on an errand of mercy, so that he might be destroyed? I would defend him.

'We have no priest here,' said I, and turned away. But I was frozen to the spot by the girl's compelling cry.

'Babs!' she shouted; 'show this rude porter what you have!'

Who could Babs be? Suddenly, there she was, right be- hind the other, with what I thought was another bicycle. But oh! (I hate using these old-fashioned and high-flown expressions, but there are no others that properly express my emotions at this instant) as I looked I became transfixed, nay, rooted to the spot. For what Babs had – and it seemed to make it worse that Babs was no less a beauty than the other, with splendid red hair instead of black – was a can- non, and it was pointed straight at the College gates! Babs looked as if she meant business, for she had a flaming lin- stock in her hand, dangerously close to the touch-hole of the cannon.

'Now,' said the dark girl, drawing a huge sword – a hor- rible two-handed weapon – from the folds of her cloak, 'will you open the gate, or will Babs blow it off its hinges, as she very well knows how to do?'

Here was student power as even our President has never

encountered it! But my mind worked with lightning swiftness. All that I had ever read of von Clausewitz came back to me in a flash: 'If the enemy's attack cannot be resisted, lure him forward, and then attack his rear.' I would admit these girls, then, and with a sudden rearward sally I would shove them and their cannon into the pool. I flung open the gate.

'Enter, ladies,' said I, with false geniality, 'and welcome to Massey College, home of chivalry and courtesy.'

But they did not rush forward as I had hoped. Babs, who really looked a rather jolly girl, turned and waved her linstock in what seemed to be a signal, and the other one – the dark one who spoke English so clumsily – cried aloud in unimpeachable Latin, 'Adeste, fideles!'

Suddenly the whole of Devonshire Place was filled with a turbulent rabble that I, still under the delusion that these were students, took to be the New Left Caucus in more than their usual extravagance of dress. Half-naked, hairy men, dirty girls whose hair blew wildly in the wind, girls carrying roses, lilies and flowers I could not identify, men carrying objects which I took to be the abortive creations of ill-mastered handicrafts, people with every sort of flag and banner – you never saw such a gang. They rushed the gate, and I was forced to retreat before them, shouting 'Stop! Wait!' as loudly as I could.

You may imagine how relieved I was to hear another voice, unmistakably English, crying 'Stop! Wait!' as well. Suddenly, right through the middle of the crowd rode a man in full armour, on a splendid horse; it is true he had a naked girl, not very effectively wrapped in his cloak, clasped in one arm, but in these permissive days such things are not unknown in our university, and whoever he was, he brought with him an atmosphere of trustworthiness that contrasted very favourably with the hostile spirit of Babs and her friend. He looked down at me, and I knew at once I was in the presence of an officer of Staff rank.

'You are the seneschal, I suppose,' he said.

'No,' I replied, 'the seneschal is at home in Leaside, and at this moment I would to God that I were with him. But I am the Master of this College, and I will defend it with all my strength, though it be but that of a poor old man, sore stricken in years; and I shall defend it also with all my art and craft, which is virtually unlimited. Now, sir, who in Hell are you?'

'It is to avoid Hell that I, and all this rabble (for I know no other way to describe most of them) seek your hospital-ity,' said he. 'I am Saint George of Cappadocia, formerly patron saint of England. This lady, with the wheel and the great Sword of Truth, is Saint Catherine of Alexandria. This other lady – the red-head with the cannon – is Saint Barbara, patroness of artillery. And we are all, every one of us here, deposed, degraded, denuded, despoiled, defeased, de-bauched, and defamed by that arch tyrant Giovanni Batista Montini, pseudonymously describing himself as Supreme Pontiff, Servant of the Servants of God, Bishop of Rome and Pope Paul the Sixth!'

There is something about other people's rhetoric that reduces my own language to the lowest common denominator. I regret my reply. It was unworthy of an academic. But history is history and truth must out.

'What's your beef?' I said.

It was the girl who shared the horse who replied. 'He means that Pope Paul announced last ninth of May that all this lot weren't really saints any more. Demoted them to legends, you see. A stinking trick, when you consider what they've been worth to the Papacy, over the centuries. But he wanted to make places for some Africans, and Americans, and other trendy riffraff. So since then we've been racketing all over Christendom trying to find someplace to stay. My name is Cleodolinda, by the way, and I'm not a saint. I just have to travel around with Georgie here because I'm a reminder of his greatest triumph. You remember, when he slew the dragon? I was the girl the dragon was – well, nowa-days they call it molesting. Will you take us in? It's All Saints, today; if we don't get a home, and a place where we are respected, before midday, it's Limbo for us, I'm afraid. And Limbo is the absolute end, you know.'

I liked Cleodolinda. As I listened, her history came back to me. Daughter of the King of Lydia. I've always got on well with princesses. But as I looked at that streetful of sanc-tified hippies and flower-children, my heart misgave me.

'Why Massey College?' I asked her. 'With all the earth to choose from, why have you come here?'

It was Saint George who answered. He never let Cleo-dolinda get a word in edgewise. The way he insisted on having all the good lines for himself, you might almost have thought they were married.

'You need us', he said, 'to balance the extreme, stringent modernity of your thinking; nothing grows old-fashioned so fast as modernity, you know; we'll keep you in touch with the real world – the world outside time. And we need you, because we want handsome quarters and you have them. It is our intention to set up a Communion of Saints in Exile, and this is the very place to do it. We wouldn't dream of going to the States, of course. But here in the colonies is just the spot.'

Cleodolinda saw that I didn't like Saint George's tone; she leaned forward and whispered, 'He's begging, you know, really; please let them in.'

Compassion overcame common sense, and I nodded. Immediately the crowd began to surge forward, and that tiresome girl Saint Catherine shouted '*Adeste fideles!*' again. I began to dislike her; she reminded me of a girl whose thesis I once supervised; she had the same quality of overwhelming feminine gall.

'One moment,' I shouted. 'It must be understood that if you enter here, I'm running the show. There'll be no taking over, do you understand? The first rule is, you must keep out of sight. I presume you are all able to remain invisible?'

'Oh, absolutely,' said Saint George; 'but we really must resume physical form for a little while each day. You've no idea how cold invisibility is, and most of us are from the East; we have to warm up, every now and then.'

'Five minutes a day,' I said, 'and I don't want you scampering all over the College. I'll tell you where to go, and there you must stay. Oh, yes, you may run along to the Chapel daily, but don't loiter. And no ostentatious miracles without written consent from the House Committee. We have participatory democracy here I'd like you to know, and that means you mayn't do anything without getting permission from the students. Now, one at a time please, and no shoving.'

Saint George helped me to check them in, and it was no trifling job. There were about two hundred of them, but the trouble was that they all insisted on bringing what they called their 'attributes' – the symbols by which they have been recognised through the ages. Saint Ursula, for instance, brought her eleven thousand virgins with her, and

insisted that they were simply personal staff, and only counted as one; they were a dowdy lot of girls, and I sent them to the kitchen, thinking the Chef would probably be able to put them to work. Saint Barbara I packed off to the Printing Room; I thought that brass cannon of hers wouldn't be noticed among all the old presses down there. Because of his association with travel I sent Saint Christopher to the parking-lot; many College people have remarked that they have never had any trouble finding a space since that moment. Saint Valentine was tiresome; he insisted that he must be free to roam at large through the living quarters, or I would regret it. I mistrusted the look in his eye. Indeed, I quickly realised that all of these saints had a strong negative side to their characters, and could turn ugly at a moment's notice. So I told Valentine to go where he liked, but that I would hold him responsible for any scandal.

Saint Lucy seemed a nice little thing, but conversation was made difficult by her trick of carrying her eyes before her on a salver. Still, she was simplicity itself compared with Saint Agatha, who walked up to me, confidently carrying her two severed breasts on a platter; I was so disconcerted that, before I grasped the full implication of my deed, I sent her to the kitchen. I made the same mistake – so full of potentialities for College cannibalism – with Saint Prudentiana, who was carrying a sponge, soaked in some jam-like substance that she insisted was martyr's blood. I can tell you that after these it was a relief to admit Saint Susanna, who carried nothing more disconcerting than a crown. As for Saint Martin, I recalled that he had once rent his cloak in two, in order to share it with a beggar, so I knew that he had experience in tearing up rags, and sent him down to our Paper-Making Room. Nor was Saint Thomasius a problem: I knew that his knack was for turning water into wine, and I thought he could make himself useful in the bar.

In fairness I must say that I foresaw certain problems that did not arise. Saint Nicholas, for instance. I was sure he would miss children, but he assured me he did not care if he never saw a child again this side of the Last Judgment; he said he wanted to re-establish himself as what he originally was – a treasurer, an administrator, a dealer in money. I shipped him straight off to the Bursary, and I understand he has since made himself very comfortable in that grandfather's clock.

Many of the saints had animals, and these gave me a lot of trouble. Saint Hubert, for instance, had brought a large white stag, which was interesting enough because it bore a blazing cross between its horns; I told him to put it to work cropping the croquet lawn, but not to let it nibble the flowering shrubs. But then there was Saint Euphemia, who had brought a bear, and knowing how bears love to catch fish, I was worried about what Roger would think; we finally made a deal that if the bear would chase those squirrels that eat all our crocus bulbs, it could stay. But the problem presented by these animals is that their powers of invisibility are not under such control as those of their saintly owners, and I don't want that bear to turn up unexpectedly in – well, for instance, in a quorum of university presidents. You may

imagine I was glad to face such easy decisions as that of Saint
Dorothy with her basket of fruit and flowers – very handy in
the private dining-room. And when Saint Petronilla turned
up with her dolphin, I simply gestured her toward the pool.
Dragons were a perfect nuisance. An otherwise decent fellow named Saint Germanus of Auxerre wanted to bring in a
dragon with seven heads. I asked him to wait. But then along
came that detestable Saint Catherine of Alexandria, with a
very nasty dragon which she insisted was not a dragon at all.

'Is a pet, a symbol of all that is evil in my nature, which I
have utterly subdued,' she said. But the dragon did not look
as subdued as I should have liked, and we had high words.
She wanted to have the Round Room all to herself and she
wanted a priest always with her; she had some extraordinary
plans for examinations: but I insisted that she scramble up
the tower, and accommodate herself in our Saint Catharine
bell, with her great spiky wheel, and her gigantic Sword of
Truth, and her disgusting dragon.

'But I am patroness of all scholars,' she protested.

'You'll see them to great advantage from up there,' I
replied, and refused to budge. She went off in a sulk.

It was with Saint George I had the worst trouble. Not
only did he insist on bringing in his horse, but he also had a
perfectly frightful dragon with him. I had to put my foot
down.

'But it isn't a dragon,' he shouted; 'it's a dog. Watch,
now. Sit, Rover!' he cried. But the dragon did not sit. It
leapt up at me and snuffled me intimately and licked me,
and tore the leg of my pyjamas, and uttered the most horri-
fying howls. Mind you, this was not wholly surprising. I
have known scores of Englishmen who owned nasty, rough,
smelly dragons that they insisted were really dogs. But this
was too much.

'That's no dog,' said I, and gave the dragon a kick in the
cloaca. 'It's blowing fire out of its nose. See – it's scorched a
great hole in my dressing-gown.'

'Of course,' he said, haughtily; 'it's a fire-dog.'

This was the last straw. 'All dragons to the furnace-room immediately,' I shouted. 'In the morning Professor Swinton will examine them, and if they are really prehistoric animals, he will take them to the Museum.' They saw I meant it, and the dragons slithered and puffed off down the stairs.

At last the whole tribe of refugee saints was disposed of about the College somehow, and I was able, in a very slight degree, to recover my composure. But then I saw that Cleodolinda had been left behind. Saint George, a real Englishman, had been so concerned about his dog he had forgotten his girl.

'Well, young woman, what are we going to do with you?' I said.

'Oh, I suppose it's Limbo for me,' she replied in a resigned but not a complaining tone. 'I'm only an attribute, you see, not a saint, and as you've put Georgie on to help the Porter he won't have time for me. After all, I can't hang about the lodge undressed like this.'

I looked at her. She repaid looking at, but I felt our Massey College men were not quite ready for so much feminine beauty, all at one gaze, so to speak.

'I don't like to think of you in Limbo,' said I, 'but the

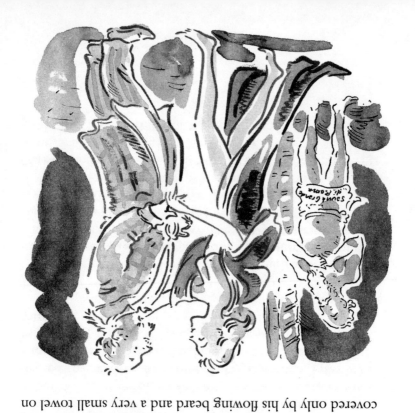

College is crammed with your friends and their luggage and pets. So – for a while, anyhow – you may use my guest-room.'

Never trust a woman. 'Oh, you *are* kind,' she said, and hopped up and down with delight, producing a very agreeable effect. 'And you won't mind if I bring a friend, will you?'

'It depends,' said I, 'a beheaded virgin or something of that kind would be all right, but no young men. I'm expected to set an example.'

'Well, it's a man, but not a bit young,' said she. 'It's Saint Patrick, you see. The poor old sweet never thought he would be desanctified, and just when the Pope pronounced his sentence he was in one of the steam baths in Rome, and he hadn't a minute to pick up a few things, so he hasn't even an attribute to bless himself with, and –'

You know how it is. Women always overdo explanations. As Cleodolinda spoke a forlorn figure hobbled forward out of the darkness beyond our gate; a shrivelled little old fellow, covered only by his flowing beard and a very small towel on which was embroidered, in red, *Sauna Grande di Roma*. He was talking long before Cleodolinda had finished.

'Yez'll have pity on me, I know,' he said, 'seeing as how I'm a fella-Celt. Sure, amn't I a Welshman meself? Isn't it well-known I sailed from Wales to Ireland on a millstone, to convert them heathen? And wouldn't I have brought the millstone itself if that dirthy ould double-crosser in Rome had give me a minute? But awww, no! It was "Out with Saint Pathrick", and no two ways about it. You'll notice that Saint Andrew is safe and snug, right where he was. Leave it to the Scotch to get it all their own way. And that roaring ould tough, Saint David, is still in his place – aw but I forgot, he's a Welshman like yourself – I mean like ourselves. Things haven't been so bad with me since the last Englishman sat on the throne of Peter, and that's damned near six centuries. You've got to let me in. I'm just a poor roont old fella like yourself –'

Here I noticed Cleodolinda kick him on the shin, and he hastily changed his tactics.

'I mean to say, a fine young lad, just in the flower of his splendour, like yourself, isn't going to turn me away, and Limbo gaping before me. You wouldn't have it on your soul. And you've a giant of a soul. I can tell by the kindly light in your eyes.'

And so on. Much, much more. And the upshot was that I sent him off with Cleodolinda to my guest-room, with strict orders not to manifest themselves in the flesh except when they were safely locked in the bathroom.

But you know how people are. Especially people who have been used to having their own way (not to speak of adoration and prayers addressed to them) for over a thousand years. It worked for a few days, and then those two were prancing around in there, quite naked, waving to Saint Catherine up in the tower, whistling at the stag, and stirring up the bear by shooting pins at it with an elastic. And the Fellows, as they sit at their breakfast, have been ogling.

If it is Patrick they see, I presume they take him for a rather more than ordinarily demented visiting professor. But from the light in my young friend's eye, I have a feeling it is Cleodolinda.

And now they are in, how shall I ever get them out?

Beware of compassion!

Robertson Davies

Robertson Davies was able (with difficulty) to provide a refuge for his insulted saints. No such refuge is available to Her Majesty Queen Elizabeth II on the annual occasion of the opening of Parliament. Her Majesty has spoken at almost every opening of Parliament since her accession in 1953, and because her words were not truly her own but those put into her mouth by the government of the day, this has, not surprisingly, gained her a reputation for duty and dignity rather than for wit.

At the public celebration of her Golden Wedding anniversary at the Banqueting House in Whitehall in 1997, however, the Queen's essential humour and charm shone through.

Golden wedding

Prime Minister, ladies and gentlemen: when Prince Philip and I were married on this day fifty years ago, Britain had just endured six years of war, emerging battered but victorious. Prince Philip had served in the Royal Navy in the Far East, while I was grappling, in the ATS, with the complexities of the combustion engine and learning to drive an ambulance with care.

Today, Prime Minister, we accept your generous hospitality in a very different Britain. The Cold War is over and our country is at peace. The economy in your charge, and which you inherited, is soundly based and growing. And, during these last fifty years, the mass-media culture has transformed our lives in any number of ways, allowing us to learn more about our fellow human beings than, in 1947, we would have thought possible.

What a remarkable fifty years they have been: for the world, for the Commonwealth and for Britain. Think what we would have missed if we had never heard the Beatles or seen Margot Fonteyn dance; never watched television, used a mobile telephone or surfed the Net (or, to be honest, listened to other people talking about surfing the Net). We would never have heard someone speak from the Moon; never have watched England win the World Cup or Red Rum three Grand Nationals. We would never have heard that Everest had been scaled, DNA unravelled, the Channel tunnel built, hip replacements become commonplace. Above all, speaking personally, we would never have known the joys of having children and grandchildren.

As you say, Prime Minister, since I came to the throne in 1952, ten Prime Ministers have served the British people and have come to see me each week at Buckingham Palace. The first, Winston Churchill, had charged with the cavalry at Omdurman. You, Prime Minister, were born in the year of my Coronation. You have all had, however, one thing in common. Your advice to me has been invaluable, as has that from your counterparts, past and present, in the other countries of which I am Queen. I have listened carefully to it all. I say, most sincerely, that I could not have done my job without it.

For I know that, despite the huge constitutional difference between a hereditary monarchy and an elected government, in reality the gulf is not so wide. They are complementary institutions, each with its own role to play. And each, in its different way, exists only with the support and consent of the people. That consent, or the lack of it, is expressed for you, Prime Minister, through the ballot box. It is a tough, even brutal, system, but at least the message is a clear one for all to read. For us, a Royal Family, however, the message is often harder to read, obscured as it can be by deference, rhetoric or the conflicting currents of public opinion. But read it we must. I have done my best, with Prince Philip's constant love and help, to interpret it correctly through the years of our marriage and of my reign as your Queen. And we shall, as a family, try together to do so in the future.

It often falls to the Prime Minister, and the government of the day, to be the bearer of the messages sent from people to sovereign. Prime Minister, I know that you, like your predecessors, will always pass such messages, as *you* read them, without fear or favour. I shall value that, and am grateful for your assurances of the loyalty and support of your government in years to come. I wish you wisdom and God's help in your determination that Britain should re-

main a country to be proud of. And, as one working couple to another, Prince Philip and I hope that on 29th March 2030 you and your wife will be celebrating your own Golden Wedding.

And talking of the future, I believe that there is an air of confidence in this country of ours just now. I pray that we, people, government and Royal Family, for we are one, can prove it to be justified and that Britain will enter the next millennium, glad, confident and a truly United Kingdom.

This, too, is an opportunity for Prince Philip and me to offer, in the words of one of the most beautiful prayers in the English language, our 'humble and hearty thanks' to all those in Britain and around the world who have welcomed us and sustained us and our family, in the good times and the bad, so unstintingly over many years. This has given us strength, most recently during the sad days after the tragedy of Diana's death. It is you, if I may now speak to all of you directly, who have seen us through, and helped us to make our duty fun. We are deeply grateful to you, each and every one.

Yesterday I listened as Prince Philip spoke at the Guild-hall, and I then proposed our host's health. Today the roles are reversed.

All too often, I fear, Prince Philip has had to listen to me speaking. Frequently we have discussed my intended speech beforehand and, as you will imagine, his views have been expressed in a forthright manner. He is someone who doesn't take easily to compliments but he has, quite simply, been my strength and stay all these years, and I, and his whole family, and this and many other countries, owe him a debt greater than he would ever claim, or we shall ever know.

Prime Minister, thank you for helping us to celebrate a very special day in our lives.

HM the Queen

The Queen is not herself a tennis player. By 'tennis' I mean, of course, real or royal tennis played today by Her Majesty's son Prince Edward, and in the past by such ancestors as Prince Albert and the most famous of royal real tennis players, King Henry VIII. With its arcane vocabulary involving phrases like 'better than half a yard', 'cutting to the chase' and 'hazard the door', tennis is a treasure-trove and a minefield for the after-dinner speaker, as the writer Margaret Scott found when venturing onto Australia's oldest court in the Royal Tennis Club in Hobart, Tasmania, in 1999.

The printed record of her speech that I have contains an early aside – 'I shall now slip in an anecdote which I trust you'll not have heard before. Dr Watson and Sherlock Holmes . . .' – but then leaves a space for the tale. Fortunately, I know it, though I'd love to know where it came from – certainly not from Conan Doyle.

Holmes and Watson are lying down at night on Dartmoor while searching for the elusive Baskerville dog when Holmes says, 'Watson, my dear fellow, look up and tell me what you see'; and Watson looks up, draws on his pipe, thinks for a moment and says, 'I see stars.' So Holmes says, 'My dear chap, you can do better than that'; and Watson says, 'Well, there's Orion and I can see Betelgeuse and Alde-

baran and . . .' Holmes is now quite exasperated and says angrily, 'Come, come, Watson, what do you deduce from what you're seeing?' Watson thinks long and hard and finally says, 'It's a fine night, Holmes.' To which Holmes responds, 'You damn fool, Watson. Someone's stolen our tent.'

The rest of Margaret Scott's speech to the tennis players of Tasmania went like this.

Royal, real and republic

The game seems to have originated in the cloisters of French monasteries, along with other rather surprisingly un-monastic benefits to humanity like Benedictine and Chartreuse. Originally it was played with the open hand instead of a racket and was known as *jeu de paume*, or palm-play. The sporting monks were soon spotted by various young French knights who took up the game with a will and began to spread it around Europe. There is a record of 'tenys' – a name taken from the server's call of 'tenez' – being introduced to Florence in 1325 and by the late four-teenth century it was established in England, where, as in France, it became popular with the upper crust and royalty.

In 1516, for instance, there is a record of 'blue velvet' pur-chased to make a 'tennis-coat' for King Henry VIII, who later had what is now the oldest royal tennis court in the world built at Hampton Court Palace. James I in 1599 referred to the game in his writing, while his eldest son, Prince Henry, died from a chill thought to have been caused by getting overheated during a tennis-match. So royal the game certainly was.

The game played by King or Prince Henry was pretty close to modern royal tennis. By the middle of the sixteenth century, at least, rackets were introduced 'woven with strings such as are found on the six-string lyre', though whether these strings were ever actually strummed, on or off the court, I can't say. Whatever the case, up until the 1870s royal tennis dominated tennisdom. Before that there are a few scattered references to 'field tennis,' played in the open air in an unenclosed space, but royal tennis was real tennis without doubt.

Lawn tennis began to forge ahead only when western inventors realised what could be done with rubber. The hard ball of real royal tennis wouldn't bounce on grass, but the invention of a rubberised bouncing ball changed every-thing. 'It is melancholy,' lamented the *St James's Gazette* in 1888, 'to see a word which has held its own for centuries gradually losing its connotation. Such a word is "tennis", by which nine persons out of ten today would understand the game of recent invention played on an unconfined court.' There were other laments as well: 'As with horsy women,' complained *Blackwood's Magazine*, 'tennisy girls become intolerable nuisances to their neighbours.' But nothing could halt the march of lawn tennis. It

swept the world. It arrived in Tasmania where prosperous orchardists, who built the house in which I now live on the Tasman Peninsula, laid out a tennis court in their garden. When I first moved in, neighbours kept coming round and saying, 'Mrs Jenkins, you know, had this place immaculate'; and then they would look at the ropy stretch of grass on which we play croquet for idiots and say bitterly, 'she had a tennis court and everything.'

After centuries of domination, then, real royal tennis is now much less widely played or known than the Mrs Jenkins variety. Moreover, looking back, you can see that, even in its hey-day, the sport has not always had an easy ride. It has, in fact, been repeatedly attacked for a whole clutch of fascinating reasons, and at some points has been declared illegal.

First, it has been condemned for promoting quarrels. Take the word bandy. This is a slippery term, as I know all too well. When I first arrived in Tasmania I heard about the bandicoot and inquired what it was. A mischievous person reminded me that a coot is a small black waterbird like a moorhen. 'Well,' he said, 'in Tassie coots have bandy legs.' I actually believed this for some years. But to resume – to bandy appears to have come into English meaning 'to strike a ball to and fro in tennis' but soon took on a wider, darker sense: to contend, strive, fight. The tennis court, then, was seen as a hot-bed of strife.

Conversely, tennis was condemned as a frivolous, un-manly pastime which distracted young men from serious military exercises. You may remember that Shakespeare showed young Prince Hal being idle and dissolute in the *Henry IV* play, and the Prince at one stage chatting about tennis in Mistress Quickly's pub. Later, of course, Hal turns over a new leaf, puts tennis behind him, and emerges in *Henry V* as the ideal warrior king. Which is why he is not at all pleased when the Dauphin, son of the King of France, sends him a gift of tennis balls. He sees the gift as a deadly insult, a suggestion that he is still the lightweight, frivolous

young fellow he once was. And he scorns the insolent gift in a famous speech:

When we have matched our rackets to these balls,
We will in France, by God's grace, play a set
Shall strike his father's crown into the hazard.
Tell him he hath made a match with such a wrangler
That all the courts of France will be disturbed
With chases.

Which is probably the most extended set of puns on the terminology of royal or real tennis ever written, and led, of course, to Laurence Olivier doing a lot of galloping.

Another reason for looking rather darkly on tennis lay in the onlooker's feeling that it was all a very chancy business, that you could never tell where the ball would end up, that the tennis court represented an anarchic world ruled by cruel Fortune rather than one watched over by divine Providence. Perhaps there have been times when you have felt like this. Anyway, the playwright Cyril Tourneur wrote in a moment of passion:

Drop out mine eye-balls and let envious fortune
Play at tennis with 'em.

Still more alarmingly, tennis was, of course, a foreign game. It was associated with Italy where, during the Renaissance period, leading families like the Borgias were mixed up in some very nasty sex scandals and seemed to be always trying to poison each other. And it had come from France. The French, even before the recent scrimmage over sewage, have never been popular in Britain. There has always been a worry about what a nice young Englishman might pick up in Paris – at best a taste for silly fashions, at worst a dose of what was known rather unfairly as the French disease. So says Sir Thomas Lovell, in yet another Shakespeare play (*Henry VIII*):

> They must . . . leave those remnants
> Of fool and feather that they got in France . . .
> . . . renouncing clean
> The faith they have in tennis and tall stockings . . .

There is, however, no doubt that the main reason for denunciation of real royal tennis is that it has been seen over the centuries as immensely, undeniably SEXY. The original French name – palm-play – told it all. The game became linked in the popular imagination with groping hands, furtive hands, hands pressed secretly together. So Rice in his *Invective Against the Vices* of 1579 condemns bowling, dicing, carding, tennising and such like deeds and acts of the flesh; while poets turn repeatedly to tennis-references in their love poetry. The Earl of Surrey, for instance, writes how his eyes are so dazzled by gleams of love that he has oft missed the ball. Something which, I hope, does not oft happen to you.

Tennis, of course, makes you hot, which meant, perhaps, stripping off your shirt, which could, in turn, lead to anything. In John Webster's marvellous play, *The White Devil*,

Duke Brachiano admits to going to his mistress's house to shift his shirt when he retires from tennis – and everyone of course knows what that means.

And heat – especially hot hands, hot palms – was in the seventeenth century and long before linked with the heat of desire. Desdemona's hot moist hand feeds Othello's suspicion of her infidelity, and another of Shakespeare's jealous husbands mutters 'Too hot, too hot!' when he sees his wife 'paddling palms and pinching fingers' with his best friend. Admittedly, neither Othello nor Leontes says anything about tennis, since women, although they may have pre-occupied the players, didn't actually appear on any kind of tennis court until the nineteenth century.

Now, of course, things are very different. Women are admitted to this excellent Club and make full use of its splendid facilities. They will next year feature prominently in the Olympics – though not, unfortunately, as real royal tennis players. Moreover, since the attempt to change our constitution so that Australia would become a republic has failed, it might have been expected that a woman – the Queen – would open the Olympics.

I shall say little about the republic – my third R – since we've probably all heard quite enough on the subject for the moment. I'd just like to leave you with a rather happy thought produced by H. G. Nelson, as a way of soothing disappointed Republicans while satisfying the most rampant of Monarchists. His idea was that John Howard, our Prime Minister, should open the games dressed as the Queen. If Mr H. were then to engage in a few exhibition bouts of real royal tennis with Malcolm Turnbull, John Clark, and Bronwyn Bishop dressed as Henry VIII, the widespread popularity of this ancient sport would be assured and the 2000 Olympics etched forever in the national memory.

Margaret Scott

Ladies and gentlemen, I have digressed once more. In my anxiety to create a nonchalant, effortless indeed, leap from the Master of Massey College to the Queen, and thence to royal sports, I have missed out Brian Johnston. Inexcusable. I was told by his son, Barry, that the very best of Brian was a speech he made to the Lord's Taverners, a charitable organisation much given to dinner and subsequent telling of tales, spinning of yarns and swapping of stories. Alas, the Taverners had no records of this speech, so, instead of giving a verbatim report of a single Johnners story, I give you the following tribute to a man whose life was lived almost entirely as if it was a particularly jolly story told after a particularly convivial dinner. Pass the port, ladies and gentlemen, and consider the life of Brian.

An evening with Brian Johnston

He comes on stage to the strains of Haydn Wood's 'Horse Guards, Whitehall', the signature tune of *Down Your Way*, which the BBC, to his annoyance, had dropped after his departure. The march, obviously familiar to an audience who knew and loved the programme, is entirely right for him – perky, comforting and terribly English. It also has a hint of brassy oompah-pah which suggests music hall and variety. After a few bars the applause begins and if you close your eyes you can visualise him entering left and making his way to the solitary stool on stage. (It's now in his study in St John's Wood.)

He doesn't quite give his trademark hornblow, but there are some mild trumpetings before he manages to articulate, 'Thank you. Thank you very much and how nice to be in Canterbury. And how nice to see the names Huddle and Freeman on the sports shop just as I came to the theatre.'

This is deft professional stuff. There's nothing worse than hearing some tired old performer who has no idea where he

is. I suspect Brian didn't go anywhere near Huddle and Freeman on his way to the theatre. He would have remembered it was the local sports shop and he would have taken the trouble to make sure they were still in business.

Now comes the first joke:

'I have to admit this . . . I had to stop just now saying "Hello Canterbury!" . . . I've got in this terrible habit . . . wherever I am, it can be Bournemouth, Manchester, Birmingham, I say hello to the town, you see, and I've got to be very careful because next week I'm going across to the Isle of Wight and I'm speaking to the ladies' luncheon club at Cowes . . . I've got to be a little bit . . .'

The end of the sentence is drowned in the first gust of gratifying laughter. 'Cowes' had been given an emphatic signpost and the audience had understood what he was saying. Not terribly difficult. Nor, on paper, terribly funny. Indeed it was the Johnston chortle which came immediately afterwards which seems to have made them laugh almost as much as the corny joke itself. 'Laugh and the world laughs with you . . .'

Then he tells the joke about last night's speech. There was this drunk who came up to him and said that it was the most boring speech he'd ever heard in his life, whereupon the chairman, not hearing what he had actually said, took Brian on one side and told him, 'Don't worry about him, he only repeats what everyone else is saying.'

More laughter. Putting yourself down is a sure-fire winner. No one in the audience will believe that this really happened to Brian, much less the previous evening, but he uses it to explain that he's feeling rather diffident about this evening and if he seems nervous this is why. He sounds – and I'm sure looks – utterly self-assured, but this is an effective way of winning your audience round, though this audience is very obviously on his side already.

'Marvellous to see so many people . . . I don't know . . . must be a very bad night on the telly or something.'

Another appreciative ripple. Other broadcasters have remarked to me that Brian often broke one of the first rules of public speaking, which is always to complete your sentence. He, however, was the past master of the phrase left hanging in the air. Since everyone always knew how his sentences were going to end, it didn't matter that he didn't always finish them. And there's no doubt that it made him sound more natural and conversational.

Then comes the story about his friend who spoke to an audience of only one chap. (Most men in Brian's stories are 'chaps'.) When he'd finished he said to the one-man audience that he was now leaving, to which the chap replied, 'Please don't go – I'm the second speaker.'

'Oi!'

But they laughed.

A brief pause and then the theme for the evening. 'How lucky I am and how much fun I've had . . . wonderful family . . . mother and father . . . sister and two brothers . . . how close we've always been . . . that was great.'

Eton scores two anecdotes. There's the William Douglas-Home one when he is confronted with an exam paper which asks him to write as succinctly as possible about (a) Socialism and (b) Coal. To which the playwright answers with the single word 'Smoke'.

'He got ten out of ten, which wasn't bad.'

The other story was the Anna May Wong joke. House-master, infatuated with famous Chinese star; phone rings; senior boy (Martin Gilliat, later the long-serving major-domo at the Queen Mother's Clarence House) answers; returns looking doleful: 'Sorry sir, Wong Number.'

Did it ever happen? I doubt it. But who cares?

On stage Brian mumbled Gilliat's name, on the grounds perhaps that his audience might not have recognised it, and sums up, fast, 'That was Eton ... then there was Oxford where I read History and P. G. Wodehouse ... played cricket six times a week.'

Then the story of scoring the try in the macintosh. And that was Oxford.

Eton Two, Oxford One.

Then comes coffee, which rates one anecdote – the one with the office manager ticking him off for not being in at nine-thirty. This scores agreeably high on the laugh scale but quickly makes way for the Grenadiers ('Best regiment in the British Army'). He kicks this off with the story of the commanding officer welcoming a new subaltern with enticing tales of drink and sex. The words are much the same as usual, except that Brian has decided to attribute the incident to a friend of his who had just joined the Hampshire regiment in Sherborne. Apart from being an unwarranted slur on a respectable old county regiment, Sherborne is in Dorset, so Brian's 'friend' would presumably have joined the Dorsets. It doesn't matter. It gets a laugh, but it's another good example of trying to pretend that an obviously ancient chestnut is a true story. No one believes it, but somehow it makes the antiquity of the joke more palatable. The laughter suggests the ploy is working.

'Only speak if you can add to the picture,' he says before telling his audience about the Queen and Prince Philip returning from a tour of Australia in 1954 and how Brian and Richard Dimbleby planned their relative tasks. Dim-bleby was on Westminster Pier waiting for *Britannia*, so they agreed he would paint a picture of the children with their Union Jacks, the Queen Mother, the corgis, 'Lord Lieutenants – all these sort of people, y'know' . . . (He likes to slip in 'y'know' from time to time, partly as verbal punctuation and partly because it increases the sense of complicity which is vital to this show's success.) After the Royal couple had disembarked, Dimbleby kept up his commentary, following the Irish State Coach halfway down Whitehall where, metaphorically speaking, Brian picked it up with a detailed description of the said coach, its history, size, appearance and so on.

'And so the great day arrived . . .' The trouble was the Queen was late; Dimbleby was lost for words and to his horror Brian heard him say, 'So as she hasn't arrived yet I'll tell

you all about the Irish State Coach.' Which he did. Thirteen tons, given to Queen Victoria, solid gold . . . 'All that sort of thing.' ('All that sort of thing' is another of his conversational tics. In other commentators the phrase might be considered sloppy, but somehow it fits Brian like a glove.) Still the Queen hasn't arrived, so Dimbleby starts to describe the horses, one by one in detail. (Brian is spinning this story out, giving it much more detail and depth than the earlier staccato gags and one-liners.) 'I was going mad by now.' He had nothing left to say. So when Dimbleby handed over to him, as planned, halfway down Whitehall, he remained virtually mute.

'And do you know, the next day people said to me, "You did the best television commentary I've ever heard. Better than Richard Dimbleby." And I realised why, because when they came past me I watched them . . . and they went past me, and I watched on my monitor as they drove into Trafalgar Square, turned left under Admiralty Arch, went about two hundred and fifty yards up the Mall, and as they approached Buckingham Palace I said, "Over now to Barclay Smith in Buckingham Palace." '

Huge laughter and applause.

'That's all I said, but what else could I say?' asks Brian through the clapping. 'They knew the Queen, they knew Prince Philip, they knew the horses, they knew the escort, they knew all about the Irish State Coach . . . so that was the lesson which I don't think many people follow nowadays. They perhaps talk too much, but there we were, that was that. And I learnt another thing from that television time . . .'

These stories are not unfamiliar – at least to me and to serious Johnston fans – but he tells them amusingly with enough colour to transport the listener back to the early fifties and those grand ceremonial occasions in the streets of London when the voices of men like himself and Richard Dimbleby really did seem to speak to the nation in the muted mellifluous tones of the officer class which was what the BBC was all about. John Birt wouldn't have got past the commissionaire!

He spends quite a lot of time talking about the differences between radio and television, about interviewing techniques, the signals given by studio managers. He lifts the veil a little, explaining arcane bits of broadcasting jargon and always injecting little bits of colourful anecdote spiced with corroborative detail – talking about the jet engine at an exhibition in the Horticultural Halls, the first match of the 1952 Indian cricket tour in Worcester and interviewing Mr Gupta ('Are you a selector?' 'No, I'm a Christian'), Uffa Fox at the Boat Show and coping with his French wife ('Only three things worth doing in life – eating, drinking and making love – and if you talk during any of them you're wasting your time').

We have only been going a few minutes and yet already, it strikes me, we have covered an enormous amount of ground, dropped an almost Nigel Dempsterish quantity of names and elicited a gratifying lot of laughter. There are critics of Brian who suggest that he was all charm, veneer and froth, but on the evidence of the evening so far, he scores surprisingly high on content. What's more, the jokes aren't just jokes for jokes' sake in the manner of some after-dinner speakers and stand-up comics; they are, most of them anyway, jokes and anecdotes which illustrate the point he is trying to make. Nothing in the performance is particularly profound, but then why should it be? – it's an entertainment, not a sermon.

Now come famous mistakes – first Henry Douglas-Home, the nightingales in the grounds of Hever Castle and the girl saying 'If you do that again Bert I'll give you a smack in the kisser' (there *is* something inherently funny in the voice of Brian chortling out 'smack in the kisser'); and second, lying under the train outside Victoria station when the loo flushed. (People laugh inordinately when Brian says 'washing their hands' with a naughty Max Miller inflection and what I imagine is a naughty-boy expression which tells you exactly what he really means.)

Wynford Vaughan-Thomas, the *Ark Royal* and the Queen Mother; Robert Hudson and the Queen at Lord's; Brian himself at the Prince of Wales's wedding, when he said 'Up the steps into the pavilion' when he should have said 'cathedral'; John Snagge stories involving HMS *Vanguard*, Len Hutton – 111 not ill, Lord Keith and the copulating couple, and, of course, the Boat Race; Max Robertson and the Queen of Norway; Audrey Russell and the Queen's 'dark black'; Stuart Hibberd and 'interlush with Ernest Lewd'; Henry Riddle and the Queen going round the bend; the Queen Mother, Princess Margaret and the boil on the bum in the hospital ward; the farting of the Queen's horse during the State visit; Brian on stage with the Crazy Gang; singing 'Underneath the Arches' with Bud Flanagan; suck-ing a lemon with Jimmy Edwards; the interview from the pillar box; being hypnotised (a rare absence of laughter); 'How's your uncle?' on the steps of the Criterion Theatre.

The voice is beginning to sound a bit tired by now, so it's a relief to pause while he plays a medley of tapes of 'Let's Go Somewhere' compiled by his son Barry. This consists of the bareback riding at the circus, being turned upside down by the blonde lady at the Chiswick Empire, the motorbike ride with 'Mad Johnny Davis', the rather tardy relighting of the Piccadilly illuminations in 1949 – 'they had to repair all the things, I think'.

And so to *Down Your Way*, with a sudden note of near seriousness: 'A great programme to do though, this, because you read in the papers, quite seriously, about awful things like famine and rape and bombings and all the stuff that goes on round the world, but if you came round Great Britain with me, as I did for fifteen years, you realise still what a mar-vellous nation we are. Everybody, in every place, seemed to be doing things for other people . . . all these people doing things for other people and it didn't get in the papers, ever. It's good news but it doesn't. So we are still a marvellous nation and I was very lucky to meet so many of 'em.'

This is the nearest, during the evening, that Brian ever comes to philosophising, and, even if, on the page, it might have a sugary look, it is very much the heart of Brian speaking. This notion of everybody doing as they would be done by was what he most earnestly believed, and you feel, listening to him, that the sentiment encompassed that night's audience – so that, even if, in reality, they were the most gruesome bunch of misanthropes and ne'er-do-wells, they were briefly transformed by Brian's magic wand into the ultimate good neighbours.

From the pudding of *Down Your Way* he picks such plums as the hundred-year-old Mrs Emily Brewster complaining that her telegram from the Queen was not in her own handwriting, and the muleteer from Usk who grew mustard and cress in his gumboots while out in India. And finally another tape recording, this one, typically, a piece of giggling – Richard Booth, the uncrowned king of Hay-on-Wye, completely unable to articulate his musical choice of 'Golden Years or anything by David Bowie' – inexplicable but entirely infectious. And then, quite briskly, Brian says that there is now an interval of twenty minutes.

Tim Heald

And so there was, after which he returned to the lectern to talk about cake and cricket.

Ladies and gentlemen, I warned you earlier of a surfeit of Oxford and, worse still, of Balliolity. Be thankful that I have not included any after-dinner stories from the University Orator, on the slightly dishonourable grounds that the best of them are in Latin. What follows is a birthday tribute from Dr Thomas Braun, a Balliol man who spent most of his life as a Fellow of Merton College, to the University Orator, Jasper Griffin, a fellow Balliol man who spent most of his life as a don at his old college. Not many such tributes are so elegantly turned, and how many speakers today can translate Latin and Greek as well as composing limericks? Pray silence for Dr Braun.

A birthday tribute to Jasper Griffin

Jasper, Miriam, friends: Miriam's request for a speech from me is a challenge. I am no Orator, as Jasper is. But I come not to bury Jasper, but to praise him – for Jasper is an honourable man. There aren't as many of those about these days as there should be. Here he stands, a brick and a rock,

*come scoglio immoto resta
contra i venti e la tempesta!*

I will do my best, for my friendship with Jasper is of even longer duration than his marriage. I recall many gatherings for coffee in Jasper's college room.

*We twa hae gimbled in the wabe,
and pu'd the gowans fine.*

We were Balliol undergraduates and joint-rotating-presidents of the Arnold and Brackenbury Society together, at

* Fiordiligi in *Così fan tutte,* Scene xi.

least I was. Together we have run with the Hare, spotted the Dick, and spread rumours about Meiggs having started the Peloponnesian War himself. Jasper now figures hugely in the fiction of Ved Mehta. I offer you one counterbalancing item of fact: the visit of Jasper with Roger Tomkys to All Souls to hear an eminent academic give his advertised lecture on the textual criticism of Lycophron's *Alexandra*. Confident that no undergraduate would dream of attending, and that his CUF requirement would thus easily be fulfilled, the scholar was hitching on his braces when there was a polite knock at his door. 'What do you want?' 'We've come for your Lycophron lecture, sir.' With less than good grace, the lecturer picked up his notes and read rapidly, only to find the two listeners maintaining their attention, making careful notes, and leaving at the end of the hour with 'Thank you: we look forward to next week.' They made him give the entire course. But by mid-term, he had come to respect them and the three became friends.†

'Jasper's coffee tastes like rubber,' said a habitué of our circle, now an eminent scientist. We came for the company. Today it tastes delicious, like the rest of the feast. That comes of Jasper's having become a Fellow of Balliol. Compare Bryson, educated at my own non-Epicurean school, who became the most Epicurean of Balliol tutors. One summer afternoon, a member of a Trades Union conference saw him seated alone in the Fellows' Garden yonder, at a table spread with spotless white napery, with a sumptuous spread in front of him, pouring himself tea from a silver teapot. The then Bursar had not been regaling the conference with the best of fare; so the Trades Unionist stepped over the low wall and asked: ' 'Ere, 'ow do I get one of them teas?' 'My dear man,' said Bryson, 'first you pass Responsions. You do

† *Ich sei, gewährt mir die Bitte,*
  In Eurem Bunde der Dritte

says the tyrant Dionysus to his two would-be assassins, moved by their constancy, at the close of Schiller's ballad *Die Bürgschaft*.

well in your exams, after which you'll find a Fellowship not too difficult; and then you ring a hand-bell for a scout.'

On the home front, Jasper has done even better. We treasure happy memories of Miriam's hospitality. She excels in domestic as well as academic virtues, as do their three daughters. (Good things often come in threes: God, the Cardinal Virtues and the Graces.) I had better not praise them too effusively, lest they hear of it and I bring a blush to the cheek of a young person (or, as P. G. Wodehouse would say, a b. to the c. of a y. p.). We miss them today; but they are bringing much-needed humane learning, Julia to the Japanese, Miranda to the Russians, and Tamara to barbarians in this island.

Jasper has grown – horizontally if not vertically. Like all of us after the age of sixteen, he has lost many brain-cells. But what excellent use he has made of those that remain! I'm not quite sure if that is wise, myself. Our friend and contemporary Tony Nuttall, sitting at his desk in his rural school years ago, was approached by another boy who said, 'My brain's better'n yourn, Tony Nuttall.' 'Oh, why?' ' 'Cos I don't use the b***** so much.' But Miriam uses hers too, so I suppose there cannot be much harm in it. The last question in next summer's last General Paper in old-style Greats Ancient History will be (I divulge this in confidence – don't tell the candidates): 'Distinguish between the work of J. and M. T. Griffin.' The answer is that J. writes about Maro and M. T. about Nero. There may be some dispute between them about which of the two perished as the greater artist. Did Maro show greater self-knowledge in ordering much of his work to be destroyed? Jasper has proved that, on balance, it was worth preserving after all. He has also written on Homer. I wrote my first essay for Michael Stokes – a tutor in Greek at Balliol whom Jasper just missed – arguing plaintively that the Homeric epics were good poetry, not just a collection of dovetailed mechanical formulae. Stokes listened good-naturedly but did not, I thought, seem fully convinced. Jasper has put the case more convincingly since then. My pupils tell me: 'As Professor Griffin has shown, Homer is good poetry . . .' I struggled in vain against our urbane Latin tutor, Gordon Williams, whose published work argued that the Roman love poets were never in love and that their poems were artificial constructs, following Greek literary models, explicable by schematic patterns of capital letters. But now my pupils tell me that Professor Griffin has proved that the Roman love poets were really in love and wrote about real girls.

So, not only in fiction, but by bringing to a misguided world an understanding of literary fact, Jasper has achieved a measure of immortality. A modern Greek might put it

differently. I have just read in a Greek travel brochure that 'Apollon so loved Iakinthos that he turned him into a flower, that he might remain forever immoral.' And now he has achieved not just the age of fifty-five – '*undena lustra*, which I understand in Pembroke College, Cambridge, is taken to mean 'wavy chandeliers' – but sixty, '*duodena lustra*', which Pembroke doubtless translates as 'splendid duodenal condition'. I like to think he may only be halfway. It was quite a time ago that a woman of Arles hit the head-lines by turning 120; she is now over 121 and has never died yet.* Newspaper-readers read with interest that as a barmaid she served Van Gogh and thought him a rude young man. (I picture his having caused annoyance by sending her an ear: 'Oh, not again: that's the third this week.')

* Jeanne Calment of Arles, born on 21 February 1875, died on 4 August 1997 aged 122 years, five months and two weeks.

There is an old lady of Arles
Whom Age is beginning to gnarl.
   She speaks well of Cézanne –
   She quite liked the man –
But when Van Gogh is mentioned, she'll snarl.

In Georgia, where birth registers were formerly not so well kept as in France, there are claims of people reaching an even greater age. A traveller was walking though a village near Tiflis recently when he saw a white-bearded patriarch weeping at his garden gate. 'What ails thee, little father?' he inquired. 'My papa has just beaten me,' was the reply. 'Impossible! How old are you, pray?' 'I am 103 and my father is 127.' 'I don't believe a word of it.' 'Very well,' said the patriarch angrily, drying his tears, 'you had better go to the church up the hill and ask the priest. He christened my father and will confirm that I'm telling the truth.'

So is Jasper '*nel mezzo del cammin di nostra vita*'? I quote from my translation of the *Inferno*:

One day, as a middle-aged hack,
I was bent on my usual track,
   When I found with dismay
   That I'd quite lost my way
In a wood that was beastly and black –

So wild and so woody that, well,
It's a story not easy to tell.
   The thought of it now
   Brings out sweat on my brow:
At the time, it was absolute hell.

It was filthy and tangled with litter:
Even death could be scarcely more bitter.
   But it did me some good
   To be lost in that wood,
And I now feel a jolly sight fitter . . .

But, no: Jasper is not entangled in a wood, if he ever was. He has achieved a remarkable degree of serenity. So he may be a little beyond halfway after all, though I should dearly love to be invited here for another delicious luncheon on his 120th birthday. But look at him: he is certainly in his prime. Without any over-sanguine actuarial estimates, we may surely apply to him the words that delighted my grandfather when, on *his* sixtieth birthday, he received a letter of congratulation from a nonagenarian beginning 'My dear young friend'. In splendid vigour, combining *gravitas* and humour in perfect proportion, he has much still to give: books and orations and lectures and apophthegms and, above all, friendship. No man can be dearer to his family and friends. A Balliol poet has written:

> From quiet homes and first beginning,
> Out to the undiscovered ends,
> There's nothing worth the wear of winning
> Save laughter and the love of friends.

I give you the toast with laughter and love: to Jasper!

Thomas Braun

And now, ladies and gentlemen, we move across the High Street to Christ Church where we find the famous cartoonist Ralph Steadman paying tribute, at the centenary dinner of the Lewis Carroll Society, to that incomparable humorist. His tour de force is introduced by Alan White.

Lewis Carroll and Ralph Steadman

Sometime in 1994, the Committee of the Lewis Carroll Society formed a sub-committee to suggest, stimulate and co-ordinate ideas for the commemoration of the centenary of the death of Lewis Carroll.

The first meeting of the 1998 Committee bristled with suggestions and those initial ideas had varying degrees of success. Some fell on stony ground: the National Film Theatre never did have a season of *Alice in Wonderland* films. Some struggled to grow, but never quite came to the fruition that we had hoped for: the Post Office at first rejected our plea for a set of Lewis Carroll stamps, but then slotted just one into a set of four Fantasy designs with C. S. Lewis and other authors.

A precious few, however, took root immediately and eventually flowered into blossoms that will live in the memory. One such was the Centenary Dinner, an idea that almost thought of itself. When?, where? and who? were questions that answered themselves. 14 January was the hundredth anniversary of Lewis Carroll's death, Christ Church was his college and home for almost half a century, and Ralph Steadman the obvious speaker.

A long-time member of the Society, Ralph, in a long and celebrated career as a cartoonist and book illustrator, has produced his own versions of Carroll's books, the *Snark* as well as the two *Alices*. He is also well-known as a broadcaster and entertainer, with a line in surrealism and nonsense to rival Carroll's own. Luckily for us, he readily and generously agreed to be our speaker.

It was a memorable evening. After dinner, Ralph stood up, donned a hat that would be the envy of the bagman in a morris side anywhere, performed his finger-slicing string trick, and – took off.

It is a mark of his generosity that, when I asked him immediately afterwards if we might have a copy of his speech for the newsletter, he simply shuffled his notes together and handed them over. So here they are, as a memento for those of us who were there, and some sort of consolation for those that weren't – financed from the proceeds of that evening.

Alan White

But we'll need some jam

My After-Dinner Speech on the occasion of the CENTENARY DINNER at CHRIST CHURCH, OXFORD on the 14th JANUARY 1998, to celebrate the LIFE of Lewis CARROLL. News of his death exactly one hundred years ago today has proved to be a gross exaggeration . . .

THE RAILWAY CARRIAGE STRING TRICK: The Opening Gambit – an intriguing attempt to engage the interest of a bored child on a long journey, or, how to gain access into the frosty omniscient world of an academic by Ralph STEADMAN. The trick with the string is performed – I mastered it in my childhood – and I am sure it is one that was quite familiar to Lewis Carroll. [TRICK] If any of you are unfamiliar with this trick please ask for a further demonstration when all formalities have been seen off the premises. I wouldn't want any of you going home with a Pillow Problem – How the devil did he do that without pulling his fingers off?? And he did it THREE times – so it must be true!

Following the trick the child would more than likely turn away and continue to gaze balefully out of the window at the passing landscape or down at Mr Dodgson's boots fidgeting restlessly amidst clouds of new-age steam heating beneath the seats. Mr Dodgson had already anticipated such a reaction and was prepared with what could be called the 'hook'. He would lean forward confidentially and whisper, 'This isn't a train you are on, you know, it's a steam-boat!'

'What?'

'A steamboat?' he repeated. Then Mr Dodgson would sit back and return his own gaze in the general direction of the carriage window and allow the puzzling thought to sow a seed of doubt.

The perplexed child would look sideways towards its mother, its nanny, butler, kidnapper – the shapeless hulk who was taking it on a long magical journey, and say, 'It's a train! Mummy, it *is* a train, isn't it? You said we were going on a train.'

'Yes dear,' replied an equally bored mother, 'it *is* a train. The kind gentleman is pretending.'

Silence would once more envelop the compartment with the claustrophobic thrum of an Egyptian Sarcophagus that had not seen the light of day for 2,000 years. There would have been no corridor. It would have been a busy train. It was the 4: 48 from Paddington and had been in service for a mere seven and a half months – a private company – GWR: Great Western Railways. The compartment was full. Six world leaders on Mr Dodgson's side and five important bankers on the facing seats with a tiny space for the shapeless hulk and the child next to the window directly opposite him.

There would be baggage and perhaps a stuffed pet Dodo precariously jammed in string net racks above their heads.

Very slowly and deliberately Mr Dodgson would ease forward again and speak quietly and deliberately, 'It *is* a steamboat. It's called the *Lady Alice*, but only you and I know that. We are sailing up the Zambezi on our way to meet Dr David Livingstone, the great explorer. He is expecting us.'

Again, Mr Dodgson would lean back and resume the implacable countenance of an Archdeacon like his father before him, as if he had merely cleared his throat politely against his hand before replacing it gently on his knee.

The child by this time would be staring intently up into the eyes of this peculiar man, which would be averted. Then those deep sad eyes would move in a sidelong glance towards the child in a playful manner and away again. The game had begun.

'But we'll need some Jam.' Mr Dodgson had leaned forward again, 'We can't go all that way without Jam. Dr Livingstone loves Jam. We *must* take him some – and lots of umbrellas too – and grand pianos! He is very musical but it rains a lot, quite suddenly.'

The child's guardian has come alive now, leans forward herself, and whispers nervously, 'Excuse me, Sir, but I believe you are bewildering the child. You are putting ideas into its head, forgive me for saying so . . .'

'And forgive *me*, Madam,' he would reply politely, raising his black top hat, 'but, on the contrary, the child is putting ideas into mine. I do apologise. Children stimulate my imagination – especially little girls, and-and-er-er. I – er – umm . . .'

At this point Mr Dodgson becomes flustered, blushes and looks uncomfortable and wei*rr*d. There would be no escape through the playful interaction with the child at this point. He must confront the adult world. He fumbles inside his pocket again and brings out a thimble on his index finger, makes it disappear, puts his hand in his pocket again, and makes it reappear.

The child's guardian remains unmoved and fixes him with an unblinking stare through features as bland and hypnotic as a 14th of January Windows 98 computer screen. Mr Dodgson crumples like a remnant of down-loaded Tweed.

'I er – t-t-try to have f-f-fun with my intellect,' he would stammer.

'What?'

'My er – intellect – it er – gets the er – b-better of me – er – and r-races ahead like a J-Jabberwock – er –.'

'A what?!' The woman is now leaning over like a subsiding Cleopatra's Needle and is in no mood to correct her lurch.

'A Jabber*what*?' said the woman, who was beginning to

grow wings and change into a wasp before his very eyes. Mr Dodgson hated wasps, particularly at picnics and especially in enclosed, stuffy railway carriages on their way to Oxford.

'A j-j-j-JABBERWOCK,' he stammered again. 'It is an imaginary b-beast, as f-far as my intellect can ascertain and it m-must be s-s-slain at all costs through and through with a vorpal sword and a s-s-snicker-s-snack!!'

'If it *is* imaginary,' replied the woman, who was now quite definitely a wasp, and her long coat had turned yellow and black, 'why bother? Since vorpal swords cost at least one thousand pounds a snicker and snacks are priceless these days, you would be wasting an awful lot of money, unless of course you have a snack with you, in which case we can *all* have a bite . . .' The woman was now hovering in front of Mr Dodgson's nose. From beneath her long yellow and black coat emerged – a Cleopatra's Needle! – a frightening sting of a thing – 'unless of courzze –', she buzzed, '*I* can have the fizzt z-z-zzting!'

Mr Dodgson glanced desperately towards the child as though looking for some kind of assistance, but, to his horror, the child, the little girl, was no longer there. Instead, there on the seat opposite lay a pot of jam, a huge pot of jam. There was plenty of jam for everyone – jam yesterday, jam tomorrow – and please let there be jam today! thought Mr Dodgson. (Our carriage door was definitely jammed when we got on the train at Paddington – so there *must* be Jam.) He looked about himself for moral support but one of the other passengers opposite had turned into a grand piano, and four of the others on his left had disappeared altogether and only four umbrellas were there, leaning against the long upholstered seat.

Mr Dodgson plunged a hand deep into his pocket again, searching for another trick. He brought out a half-eaten sandwich and offered it to the tip of the terrifying needle which was the nearest part of the gruesome creature who only a moment ago was sitting innocently next to the sweetest little girl he had ever set eyes upon, but who now alas had gone.

The hovering Waspwoman probed the limp titbit through and through, snicking and snacking ferociously and declaring. 'There's nothing in it! It is nothing but-a but-a – No BUTTER at all. Not even BUTTER!! You can't have much of a picnic without BUTTER!! What's in your other pocket? Let me zzzzee.'

Mr Dodgson put his hand lamely into his other pocket and pulled out a handkerchief.

'A tablecloth!!!' shrieked the Waspwoman. 'So you *were* going to have a picnic, but it was going to be a secret. A secret picnic with no BUTTER – butta daughter of mine would be the jam – if I am not very much mistaken!! Can you play the piano?'

'Only on M-mondays, W-wednesdays and S-s-saturdays,' said Mr Dodgson, trying to think of something clever to say, 'but today is F-friday. It always r-r-rains when I play on F-fridays.' 'Capital!' said the Waspwoman, 'and my daughter can sing. The other passengers' (who had now turned into fish with deep, sad, staring eyes and were dressed in batter, except for one who had become a Turtle with a suitcase strapped to its back) 'can hold up the umbrellas so that they won't drown. Now if you would care to open the jar and let my daughter out we can begin.'

Mr Dodgson unscrewed the lid gingerly and out clambered a very sticky little girl who was immediately licked clean by her very loving mother. 'I do so adore this part of motherhood', she said between licks, 'and particularly before it rains. I do think that rain ruins a picnic, don't you?'

Mr Dodgson nodded weakly and got up to address the piano keys, as if he were trying to remember a Postcode. 'I can only play in the key of C', he said, 'and p-perhaps in B if it's a s-simple tune.'

'Oh, NO! I HATE Beezzz,' buzzed the Waspwoman who went white all over at the very sound of the letter and, waving her sting menacingly but recovering almost immedi-ately, enquired, 'You can't play in T can you? A picnic is never complete without TEA.'

Mr Dodgson smiled as he began to enter into the spirit of things, 'I have been known to play a passable Trumpet solo on a teapot on S-sunday afternoons.'

'But if you play so LOW my daughter can't keep up. She has a very high voice. Better stick to the piano. Here's some jam. Shall we begin?'

Mr Dodgson stuck himself to the piano and began to play 'I Dreamt That I Melt In Marble Halls' and the little girl burst into a tuneless squeal like a train on rusty rails. The girl's mother hovered around the jam pot tucking in to the jam between verses. It immediately began to rain and the fish passengers rushed forward to hold the umbrellas over everyone.

'Where's the Turtle?' interrupted the Waspwoman.

'It was only a Mock Turtle, Madam,' explained Mr Dodgson with a touch of sarcasm in his voice, 'so it really wasn't here.' 'If it *wasn't* here then it weren't so it must have caught an earlier train, in which case it won't already be in Oxford – or', said the waspwoman with uncanny hindsight, 'if it *didn't* then it can't be – so it ain't!'

'Quite so!' said Mr Dodgson, who then had a try at 'She Was Poor but She Was a Hornet in a Hairnet'. The little girl, a Squire's daughter, who was used to servants and didn't know what Daddy did when he wasn't home, didn't know the words either, so the fish took over with such a melancholy sound like gargling water over slime green banknotes. It was so very very sad that everybody began to cry. Water was sloshing about everywhere. The luggage had fallen from the overhead racks and was floating and swaying in perfect harmony which is difficult since nobody was. Only the stuffed Dodo was in tune as it mumbled Dodo, Ray-ray, Mee-mee, Fah-fah, So-so, Lah-lah, Tea-tea, DO-D-o-o-o-o-O!

The Waspwoman by this time was beginning to return to her former shapeless hulk except that her face was covered in jam and her wings hung down her back like old wet copies of unsold *Punch* magazines. Hovering was quite out of the question.

When Mr Dodgson plunged into 'Abide With Me; fast falls the sinking Yen', the railway carriage was half full of water.

'You *did* say this train was a boat, did you not, Sir?' said the woman, who was washing the jam off her face as she spoke.

'A Steamboat, Madam, but only on Tuesdays, Thursdays and half a d-day on Sundays b-between the hours of nine and f-five. There are t-timetables, however, at the t-ticket office but they c-cost at least a th-thousand pounds an hour. I believe we are s-s-sinking f-f-f-f-fast, Madam, but this piano is staying afloat on account of it b-being a city gent. If you would c-care to c-climb aboard in A minor we can all s-sail into Oxford in double time to a rousing chorus of Dr Thomas ARNE's 'Rule B-B-Britannia'. Grab hold of this s-s-string, Madam. I'll p-pull you up. With any luck we shall be home for the t-teapot handle's *Water Music*, and the sun is sh-shining too so we can p-p-picnic on the lawn if you and your d-d-d-daughter would care to join me along with the other p-p-p-p-p-passengers.'

The other passengers were delighted and were already holding large invitation cards as big as suitcases on which were written the words, 'FISH ON FRIDAYS ONLY'. They turned the umbrellas upside down and leaped into them like salmon swimming upstream to sell their shares.

By the time they reached Banbury everyone had brightened and stopped crying. Everyone was singing – the umbrellas sang inside-out and the piano, in spite of being highly strung, had a fine Welsh baritone voice, came from Mold in North Wales and was turning green. They sang the compartment dry in no time but when they reached Oxford everybody squelched off the train in wet socks. But it seemed only natural somehow. There are some things in life that never dry up especially in WONDERLAND.

It ses 'ere –

– say something about string and Mock Turtles – Most remarkable of Victorian inventions. They made it from flax and hemp long before Mr Sellotape thought of string or soup. If I speak too slow, I may start speaking backwards, but if I speak fast I may just be able to catch up with myself and even finish before I do – What?

Suit of the evening – Bee-ooootiful suit.

My father was five and a half in 1898 and Picasso was sixteen.

Ralph Steadman

In the same year as the Carroll centenary Bridget Jones's fellow faithful singleton, Jude, got married. Wedding speeches are sometimes delivered after drinks or bouquets, sometimes after cake, but all are required to be felicitous, amusing and just as toasty as after dinners. My perception is that at most weddings the speech bit is pretty curate's eggy. However eloquent the majority, there's always at least one very bad apple. From what follows I sense that Bridget's perceptive creator Helen Fielding agrees.

Bridget Jones at a wedding

'It was when we moved to Great Missenden that Judith's outstanding gifts in the freestyle and butterfly strokes . . .'

By 5 o'clock Sir Ralph had already been talking for twenty-five minutes.

'. . . became *strongly* apparent not only to us, her admittedly *biased* – he looked up to elicit a dutiful faint ripple of pretend laughter – 'parents, but to the entire South Buckinghamshire region. It was a year in which Judith not only attained *first place* for the butterfly and freestyle sections in three consecutive tournaments in the South Buckinghamshire Under-Twelves Dolphin League but obtained her Gold Personal Survival Medal just three weeks before her first year exams! . . .'

'What's going on with you and Simon?' I hissed to Shaz. 'Nothing,' she hissed back, staring straight ahead at the audience.

'. . . In that same very busy year Judith obtained a distinction in her Grade II Associated Board Examinations on the clarinet – an early indication of the rounded "Femma Universale" she was to become . . .'

'But he must have been watching you in church otherwise he wouldn't have rushed up in time to catch you.' 'I know, but I was sick in his hand in the vestry.'

'. . . Keen and accomplished swimmer, deputy head girl – and frankly this, as the headmistress privately admitted to me, was an error of judgement since Karen Jenkins' performance as head girl was . . . well . . . This is a day for celebration, not for regret, and I know Karen's, er, *father* is with us today . . .'

Caught Mark's eye and thought was going to explode. Jude was a model of detachment, beaming at everyone, stroking Vile Richard's knee and giving him little kisses for all the world as if the cauchemarish cacophony were not happening and she had not, on so many occasions, slumped drunkenly on my floor incanting 'Commitment-phobic bastard. Vile by name, and Vile by nature, 'ere, 'ave we run out of wine?'

'. . . Second lead clarinettist in the school orchestra, keen trapezer, Judith was and is a prize *beyond rubies* . . .'

Could see where all this was leading. Unfortunately it took a further thirty-five-minute trawl through Jude's gap year, Cambridge triumph, and meteoric rise through the corridors of the financial world to get there.

'. . . And finally, it only remains for me to hope that, er . . .'

Everyone held their breath as Sir Ralph looked down at his notes for really beyond all sense, beyond all reason, beyond all decorum and good English manners, too long.

'*Richard!*' he said finally, 'is suitably grateful for this priceless gift, this jewel, which has today been so graciously bestowed upon him.'

Richard, rather wittily, rolled his eyes, and the room broke into relieved applause. Sir Ralph seemed inclined to continue with another forty pages, but mercifully gave up when the applause didn't.

Vile Richard then gave a short and rather endearing speech, and read out a selection of telegrams, which were all as dull as bricks apart from one from Tom in San Francisco, which unfortunately read: 'CONGRATULATIONS: MAY IT BE THE FIRST OF MANY.'

Then Jude got to her feet. She said a few very nice words of thanks and then – hurrah! – started reading out the bit that me and Shaz had done with her last night. This is what she said. As follows. Hurrah.

'Today I bade farewell to being a Singleton. But although I am now a Married I promise not to be a Smug one. I promise never to torment any Singletons in the world by asking them why they're still not married, or ever say "How's your love life?" Instead, I will always respect that that is as much their private business as whether I am still having sex with my husband.'

'I promise she will still be having sex with her husband,' said Vile Richard and everyone laughed.

'I promise never to suggest that Singletondom is a mistake, or that because someone is a Singleton there is anything wrong with them. For, as we all know, Singletondom is a normal state in the modern world, all of us are single at different times in our lives and the state is every bit as worthy of respect as Holy Wedlock.'

There was a ripple of appreciation. (At least I think that's what it was.)

'I promise also to keep in constant contact with my best friends, Bridget and Sharon, who are living proof that the Urban Singleton Family is just as strong and supportive, just as there for you, as anyone's blood family.'

I grinned sheepishly as Shazzer dug her toe into mine under the table. Jude looked round at us and raised her glass.

'And now I'd like to raise a toast to Bridget and Shazzer: the best friends a girl could have in the whole world.'

(I wrote that bit.)

'Ladies and gentlemen – the bridesmaids.'

There was a huge roar of applause. Love Jude, love Shaz, I thought as everyone rose to their feet.

'The bridesmaids,' said everyone. Was marvellous having all the attention. Saw Simon beaming at Shaz and looked across at Mark to see him beaming at me too.

Helen Fielding

Helen Fielding has created a great comic character, and much of the humour lies in the fact that Bridget doesn't realise how funny she is. Maureen Lipman, on the other hand, knows precisely how funny she can be. Yet, like Mrs Thatcher, she likes a story to have a point. When asked for an example of her own after-dinner oratory she suggested this offering, which was originally set before the supreme example of the Women who Lunch, viz. the Women of the Year Lunch at the Savoy Hotel. This is a delightful and humorous speech, but it is more than just funny . . .

BeRo and borrowed hats

There were about ten of them, although numbers changed depending on the affair. The affair could be anything from an evening of cards and bridge rolls to a meeting to devise ways of raising money for a small corner of Israel most of them would never see. The one thing the affair never was, was an affair. They all had names which dated them as specifically and nostalgically as a tin of Ostermilk dates a Baby Boomer. There was a Freda and a Nora, two Lillys and a Helen and a Jean, a Miriam and a Minnie and a Rita and also, it really goes without saying, a Zelma. They were 'The Women'. The women of my childhood. The indomitable, varied, never-changing and constant Women. The mothers

of all those Susans and Janets and Maureens and the wives of all those Harrys and Maxes and Moishes.

And they were smart as paint. Each woman had lived her twenties through a long and bloody war, which hit them personally in a way which made them shudder at the near-miss of it all. They married in utility suits and borrowed hats, and the men they married donned uniforms and left within weeks or months of their ration-book weddings. In their quiet moments all of them feared that the uniformed strangers who might return would do so with new manners and new mores to which they might not know how to rise. Some of them worked in factories and shops and aero-dromes during this time, and all of them loved the work they were doing: the companionable vivacity, the shared jokes and the pooled fears. They were good at their jobs. They were proud of their ability to contribute. They glowed with the pride that only a wage-packet with your name on it could bring.

They were even secretly saddened when the war was over and their contribution was no longer deemed necessary. But there was no question of not returning to the world of housewifery. They knew that their places were in the home and they went along with the Americanised adventurousness which showed them what a fun place the home could be when stocked with labour-saving devices and Persil's New Blue White. They all had their babies and learned to bake from the BeRo cookbook whilst listening to *Music While You Work*, and swapped one workplace for another. And they were happy comparing their kids and watching their husbands make a living and shopping daily on what he gave them weekly, and socialising with each other at synagogue functions and barmitzvahs and silver weddings. Year in, year out, putting pancake mixture in the pan and pancake makeup on their arms, to finish off their beaded evening-gowns and bouffant once-a-week hair setting. And still when we came home from school, clutching our 'Could do better if she stopped trying to entertain the class' report, they gave us beans on toast and a homemade macaroon. And so it was until the kids left home and the nest sparkled just a little less though the polish now came in spray-cans.

So you asked me, Committee Members of The Women of the Year, high-achievers to a man, what in my role has inspired me, and I think of my heroines from childhood upwards: Enid Blyton's George, and *Lorna at the Wells*, and Pauline, Petrova and Posy in *Ballet Shoes* and Joan Nicholson, a keen and sensitive English teacher, and Alma Cogan because she was a star *and* 'one of us', and Joyce Grenfell and Elizabeth Taylor and Maggie Smith and Odette Hallowes as played by Anna Neagle, and Glenys and Glenda and Aung San Suu Kyi on a daily level. And in the end I go back to the question 'What in your role has inspired you?' and I see etched instead on my retina those women in their navy or black pleated skirts with beautifully laundered, brightly patterned blouses and court shoes. Nylon stockings and firm foundations. Max Factor lipstick and shiny blue eyeshadow and carefully co-ordinated costume jewellery. The women who would never achieve what we here today have achieved: the right and the talent to succeed in what we love to do. In a month of Sunday roasts they were never going to make it to this Lunch, but by hell they were going to make sure that their Janes and Susans and their Maureens did.

I'll tell you what inspires people to succeed the world over. Encouragement and love. 'Yes, you can do it and you'll be the best'; not 'She'll never come to anything, it's the lad that's got the brains.' When 'The Women' sat round with their china cups and their slice of Madeira cake and Zelma said, 'Sing "Dreamboat" for them, Maureen, or tell them that joke about "Moon River".' ('when 'Moon River' was the punchline of the joke), the fact that not one of those strong, powdery faces registered disapproval of me and my tiny talent gave me the go-ahead to perform. And when I'd finished, their hands came together and they shouted for more. It was the warmest and most secure sound I ever knew.

Forty-six years later I take that feeling on stage with me every night. And without it I could never love my audience and expect them to reciprocate. Joyce Grenfell said there is no performance which is not a circle. I put out my hand to give but if you are not there to receive then the circle is not complete. Putting that hand out requires skill and courage and vats of vitality, but most of all it requires confidence. And the inspiration for that confidence came from a group of very ordinary, unshowy, provincial, sparky, altruistic and very inspirational ladies who didn't have the time or the credentials to lunch, except very rarely at the Kardomah.

Forgive me for dashing away from this special day but I have a matinée in Richmond and many of my audience are so old that if I keep them waiting they may not survive the afternoon.

Maureen Lipman

Which brings me to Dorset. Don't ask me why. I could say that Ms Lipman's mention of a matinée in Richmond was a reminder that I lived there for many years and attended a number of matinées in that lovely theatre on the Green. And I could suggest that my adopted Richmond made me think of my native Dorset. But that would be an untruth. Which brings me to Dorset. Coming to Dorset is, for me, as inevitable as coming to Gyles Brandreth. I was born in Dorset. I was educated in Dorset. My father was born in Dorset. I once held a scholarship for which only those born in Dorset, educated in Dorset and with at least one parent born in Dorset qualified. Because of my close association with the County of Dorset I belong to the Society of Dorset Men. The Society of Dorset Men holds regular dinners to which, alas, I have never been. It also publishes a magazine in which details of the dinners and the speeches made after them are faithfully recorded. In the latest issue I came across this charming speech. I wish I had been present to hear it, for it is full of humorous, gentle after-dinner stories about the very best of all English Counties. Ladies and gentlemen, pray silence for Mr David Burnett, publisher of the Dovecote Press, and a good sound Dorset man.

To the Society of Dorset Men

Mr President. My Lords, ladies, gentlemen: On a May day in 1971 my girlfriend, Sarah, now my wife, and I were on our way from London to a christening when we drove into the River Tarrant at the ford at Tarrant Monkton in our Morris 1000 Traveller. There was a splash, a sort of bow wave set the ducks to quacking, after which the engine spluttered and we came to an abrupt halt in mid-stream. Thus did I first come to Dorset.

For a while we just sat there, grinning stupidly, the Tarrant running gently over the pedals, as if sitting marooned in the middle of a river was the most natural thing in the

world. We were watched, as I remember, from the little seventeenth-century packhorse bridge by a couple of old codgers who, if enchanted by the shortness of Sarah's miniskirt when we finally got out and pushed, had undoubtedly seen it all before.

By chance, and I only mention it because of what's happening elsewhere in the world, we spent much of the next nine months in Afghanistan: then at peace and as welcoming as this gathering tonight. But within a year we were back in Dorset, and living in a cottage and group of farm buildings on the edge of the water meadows alongside the River Allen, a short trout stream that rises in the Gussages and joins the Stour at Wimborne. We have remained there ever since, and it's from there that the Dovecote Press has now published over two hundred books, a number that continues to grow.

In those days I didn't know my Rhyme Intrinsecas from my Hazelbury Bryans, or Piddletrenthide from Powerstock. But I suppose I sensed we'd finally arrived when shortly afterwards I was standing with one of Portland's great characters, Cecil 'Skylark' Durston, in his garden at Southwell, when with barely a by-your-leave he kissed me firmly on both cheeks. I should add, and this is important, that Skylark was then in his nineties. 'You'll not believe this,' he said, 'but two more of them and you'd be being kissed by Admiral Lord Nelson.' I looked baffled. Skylark chuckled. Finally he came clean.

As the fleet prepared for action off Cape Trafalgar in 1805 Nelson had reassuringly placed his lips on the top of the head of a frightened Portland-born powder monkey, one of the young lads on board the *Victory* who brought up the powder for the gun crews from the magazine once the first broadsides were fired and battle was engaged. Many years later, on his 100th birthday, that same powder monkey, now a celebrated old salt, and undoubtedly the most distinguished living Portlander, toured the Island in a pony and trap so that mothers could bring out their children to be kissed: as if somehow they too, and in turn, would live to a ripe old age. One of those children was Skylark, then an infant in arms, and now he in turn had kissed me.

This notion of the ways in which we can be catapulted back into the past seemed to me extraordinary, for it's a game we all can play. Then I started thinking about it. If three kisses carried me back nearly two centuries to Horatio Nelson, then a fourth, and undoubtedly much more passionate kiss, brought me into contact with the lovely if ill-fated Emma Hamilton, Nelson's mistress, to whom Nelson wrote shortly before his death: 'I can neither eat nor sleep for thinking of you. I never touch even pudding' – which of course would have meant having to decline every morsel of the wonderful meal we've enjoyed this evening. Another fourth kiss, perhaps the most famous in English history, led me from Portland to Portesham, and to Thomas Masterman Hardy, who was born in the village, and who as flag captain of the *Victory* took the mortally wounded admiral in his arms. And to whom Nelson whispered his dying words, words so well-known I don't even need to repeat them.

Suddenly there seemed no end to all this kissing, and so as to cool down, as it were, I drove home via the monument to Hardy above Portesham on top of Black Down Hill. It is, alas, and despite its size, the least distinguished of all Dorset's monuments, looking more like a factory chimney than a sailor's memorial. It was late autumn, sharp and clear. There were sloes in the hedges, a buzzard wheeled overhead. At nearly 800 feet above sea level the views were panoramic.

To the south was the Chesil. To the west lay Pilsdon Pen (which, thanks to modern surveying techniques, has now lost its crown as Dorset's highest point to its wooded 912 feet high neighbour, Lewesdon Hill). To the north was the rolling chalk downland that fills much of the heart of the country. To the east, beyond Dorchester, beyond the birth-

place of that other more celebrated Thomas Hardy, lay the heath and the distant Purbecks.

Here then was 'Dorset, Our County' at the tail end of an October day nearly thirty years ago. Of course we all of us have our favourite places. The view from Bulbarrow out over the Blackmore Vale. The tiny church at Winterborne Tomson, which sits like an upturned boat on the edge of a farmyard. Swimming at dusk on the incoming tide at Kimmeridge, when the rock ledges have been warmed by the sun. Picnicking on the ramparts of Coney's Castle, an overgrown Iron Age hillfort, with the entire Marshwood Vale spread out in front of you. Tracing the ghostly grass footprint of Vanbrugh's Eastbury House at Tarrant Gunville on the edge of Cranborne Chase, which, until it was blown up in late Georgian times, was, after Blenheim, the largest country house in England.

As for me, I can't drop down into the Tarrant Valley without thanking the Tarrant's waters for halting me where they did all those years ago. And I know that all of you share my affection for this most glorious of English counties. My Lords, ladies and gentlemen. Please charge your glasses, and join me in the toast: 'Dorset. Our County.'

David Burnett

Shortly after David Burnett's account of his kissing link with Nelson, Enid Taylor, Senior Warden of the Worshipful Society of Apothecaries and shortly to become the first Lady Master, rose to reply on behalf of the guests. She told a couple of stories I hadn't heard before about a short-staffed greengrocer who employed a boy as temporary help.

'A customer came into the shop', said Mrs Taylor, 'and asked to buy half a lettuce. The boy was a little confused about this so he went to the back of the shop to consult the owner, saying, "There is a pillock out there who wants to buy half a lettuce." At this point he realised that the customer had followed him and was standing behind him, and

he quickly added, "And this gentleman wants to buy the other half." The owner cut the lettuce in half and sold it. Later he said, "That was very bright of you, boy. Where do you come from?" "Limerick," says the boy. "Well, why did you leave Limerick?" "Boring. In Limerick you are either a rugby player or a whore." "Boy, I'll have you know my wife comes from Limerick." "Oh yes," said the boy, "and which team did she play for?'

Before I was distracted, I was saying that Dorset was the very best of all English counties. Ladies and gentlemen, I said so with sincerity, nay with the very deepest sincerity. And I did so, I venture to say, because the County of Corn-wall, which some misleadingly refer to as the Duchy of Cornwall, or even, in the words of the immortal 'Q', aka Sir Arthur Quiller-Couch, as 'The Delectable Duchy', is not a part of England but of Britain, of Great Britain, a fact which in no way diminishes . . . no sir, I will not give way, over-come though I may be by the exuberance of my own verbosity, for . . . where was I . . . ah, yes . . . Cornwall. Sermons. We have had no sermons. The after-dinner sermon does not, as far as I know, exist, the sermon serving principally as a prelude to a Sunday lunch, or, if at Evensong, then dinner. Bishop Bill preaches a mighty sermon. Mightily doth he preach and with much wit and humour also. Verily. Bishop Bill is William Ind, My Lord Bishop of Truro, and he's also crazy about cricket. Just before Christmas, in my parish church, Saint Fimbarrus of Fowey, the Bishop preached one of his mighty witty sermons, and on the way out he accosteth me and saith, 'Guess what. I've just had the most amazing experience. I made an after-dinner speech at the XL Club. I came in straight after Ted Dexter.'

And this is what he hath said.

Not enough cricket

Towards the end of his life, John Betjeman was asked if there was anything he regretted about his life and he replied simply with a chuckle, 'Not enough sex.' If I was asked the same question I would reply immediately, 'Not enough cricket; not enough playing of it, not enough watching of it, not enough reading about it.' It has been one of the passions of my life since 1952 when I was ten.

As a bishop I have had a personal audience with the Pope: I have got photographs to prove it. I have had lunch with the Queen, preached at several cathedrals, lectured at Oxford and Cambridge; but now to be here at a dinner and speaking after Ted Dexter, I can say with real zest and conviction, 'Nunc Dimittis; Lord now lettest Thou Thy servant depart in peace according to Thy word, for mine eyes have seen Ted Dexter and Hubert Doggart.'

I saw my first first-class match at Cheltenham in 1952 and saw Tom Graveney bat. He did not get many runs but, from then on, I was hooked. I do not know whether it was because all the crowd was talking about him but, from then on, I ate, drank, talked and slept Tom Graveney and, if I am honest, in a sense I still do. If I see a cricket book of that period I turn immediately to the index to look to see if there are references to him and, if there are not, I throw the book away. He has given me some of the most miserable and also some of the happiest days of my life. I remember, for instance, being overjoyed when, in the first innings of the Lord's Test against Australia in 1953, Len Hutton put on 168 and I longed for the next day when I was certain he would go to his 100. I remember running from the school dining-hall at lunchtime to hear the lunchtime scoreboard and discovering, to my horror, that he had been yorked that morning fourth ball by Lindwall and had not added to his overnight 78. Neville Cardus said, rather unkindly, that he should set his alarm clock earlier. Then there was a wonderful 100 in 1955 at Sydney, but he was in and out of the England side. Then, in 1957, he was brought back at Lord's and was out LBW to Gilchrist for nought. I was teased mercilessly at school, but got my own back at Trent Bridge at the next match when he made 258.

Then I saw every ball of his 164 at the Oval in their final Test of that year when, as you remember, the West Indies were bowled out twice for 89 and 86 by Laker and Lock and, to my mind, Graveney had beaten them almost on his own. And then, finally, that wonderful Indian summer which began in 1966 when he became what Colin Cowdrey described as steady, determined and faultless. But, by then, of course, he had moved to Worcestershire and my heart was still with Gloucestershire. And I knew that I was never going to be like Tom Graveney anyway and that what I had become was a slow left arm bowler. So my hero, inevitably, was that very different, much more earthy, marvellous character, Sam Cook, the Gloucesters' fair left arm bowler. He was held in enormous affection in Gloucestershire. I remember being at Cheltenham in 1956 or 1957, when Sam came in to bat – and bear in mind it was nearer the end than the beginning of August. He edged a ball between his legs and the leg stump from Shackleton for 4 and a few minutes later over the PA system it was announced that Sam had scored his hundredth run for the season! The game stopped, people shook hands with him including the umpires; but, of course, as I am sure Ted Dexter will bear out, when it came to bowling on a turning wicket, he and Bomber Wells were a different matter and would be getting through 23 or 24 overs to the hour. Would that that happened today.

Sam was the kind of cricketer I would have liked to be and, just about two years ago, I was in Tetbury parish church, soon after his funeral. I had not been able to go to his funeral but I know that, at that funeral, Tom Graveney gave the address and, when afterwards they walked out towards the grave, Arthur Milton had a look and said, 'Look! Look at the poor bugger; even now he's been put at third man – that's where he's being buried!' So I am grateful for these memories and these people and for numerous other matches which I have seen in my life. I think, for instance, of Fred Titmus's Benefit, Middlesex v. Sussex at Lord's at the beginning of June 1963. The weather was very hot and Sussex won by one run, though I am sorry to say that Ted Dexter did not do much with the bat; but, with his customary warmth of heart, he gave his wicket to Titmus as a Benefit present for two, caught Hooker, bowled Titmus two. So, quickly to end, the memories of it have been at the centre of my life and, if I am honest, have affected everything. I remember my history master telling me that I should read Gibbon to improve my English style. I preferred, and still prefer, Neville Cardus and, above all, Robertson-Glasgow. In all the *Decline and Fall of the Roman Empire* there is no sentence to equal one in Robertson-Glasgow's essay about Walter Hammond:

I mean the effect on a match of his presence alone, the influence on a bowler's feelings of the sight of Hammond taking guard at about 11.50 am when the lunch seemed far and the boundary near.

So I have these memories and, although I have played cricket at an infinitely lower level than anyone else on this table, I have had experiences which probably they have not. I remember playing in theological college cricket for instance, where one player argued with the umpire about the theology of LBW, having been given out in that way. He wanted to know what evidence there was that the world was not going to end at the time between when the ball hit his pad and would have gone on to the wicket. I also played, when I was Bishop of Grantham, for the Lincolnshire Gentlemen. Obviously, the people that I played with knew who I was, but that was all. I was put on to bowl just before lunch and the opposing team was about 60 for 1. For the first three balls I concentrated on bowling on a length, tried to spin the fourth – it did not turn but was a bit short. The batsman tried to cut it, got a top edge, hit the wicketkeeper on the shoulder, looped up the ball to first slip who caught it easily. The batsman was rightly furious with himself and, as he left, looked up the wicket at me and said with some venom, 'I wish I was a bloody bishop.'

I got runs and wickets when I played in a bishops' team at the Lambeth Conference in 1998, thanks, I think, to a couple of generous LBW decisions by the umpire, Robert Runcie, who had been the Archbishop of Canterbury. And I should say that a couple of the men I got out were Australians! And then, in 1997, I had moved to Cornwall – and cricket is very strong in Cornwall – and I played once or twice for the Cornish Gentlemen. But, as a matter of interest, it is worth knowing that only two Cornishmen have ever played cricket for England – Jack Richards, who kept wicket and scored 100 against Australia, and, much more important than him, the man with the unfortunate name of Jack Crapp, who played for Gloucestershire with great distinction, was a wonderful slip fielder and left-handed batsman, and who played for England several times in the late 1940s. There is a story told about him that he, with Denis Compton, won a match for England against South Africa in South Africa in 1948/9, and the headline in one of the West of England papers was, I would think, a trifle unfortunate. It said simply, 'All Englishmen take their hats off to Crapp!'

And so it is that cricket has been important to me all my life and you may wonder how I keep going. You may wonder, for instance, how I get through interminable church services. Hymn numbers are a great solace. Only last week we had hymn number 285, omitting the asterisked verses, so I thought of Peter May at Edgbaston in 1957. During Lent it is often hymn 99, and then I think of Ted Dexter among others. And so I survive and long for heaven when I shall be able to have lessons in slow left arm bowling from Sam Cook, Farmer White and Wilfred Rhodes. And then, and only then, I might get Ted Dexter out.

William Ind, Bishop of Truro

Before we leave cricket I must share with you a letter sent in by Jilly Cooper. In response to my request for an example of her after-dinner wit she sent me this anecdote about David Niven, which she says never fails to bring the house down in an after-dinner speech.

Niven was a consummate professional when it came to storytelling, as I remember when I once had to compile a magazine piece about famous people's preferred holidays and he came up with a brilliant composition in half an hour flat. My favourite story of his, however, is the one about dressing up as a goat at a fancy dress ball in Malta and squatting down to unload a handful of black olives under the nose of Lord Mountbatten, who was then commanding the Mediterranean fleet. But that's another story ... Here, for now, is Jilly on Niven on cricket and a polite lady at the BBC.

Meeting David Niven

When I was at the *Sunday Times*, I was sent to interview David Niven. This is when he wrote *The Moon's a Balloon*. Very excited, I rolled up at the Capital Hotel, and was so nervous I downed a couple of very large gin and tonics. David Niven didn't turn up and finally, slightly later when I'd rung the *Sunday Times* and he'd rung the *Sunday Times*, I discovered he'd gone to the Connaught by mistake. Several drinks later, about two o'clock, we finally met up at the Capital, and as we'd started drinking, we carried on. About five o'clock he was decanted into a taxi to do a recorded broadcast for 'Woman's Hour'.

I went back to the *Sunday Times* and to my horror realised that I had a completely virgin notebook and in the end was reduced to writing: '*The Moon's a Balloon* is one of the best books I've ever read. David Niven is the most stylish man I've ever met.' I then proceeded to write a piece about style, because I hadn't got anything else to say about him, except how wonderful he was.

A few days later, I received this wonderful letter from him:

Dear nice, beautiful, friendly and giggly Jilly,

I'm very rude, but I was pissed when we parted and I never thanked you for a delicious luncheon. I *must* have been pissed if I let you pay!

Thank GOD you didn't come with me into the BBC. It was a shambles. A nice prim lady interviewed me on Woman's Hour . . . an interview of unparalleled dreariness until she said: 'You mention the Hollywood Cricket Club in your book – do you have many happy memories of our National Game?'

Niven (smirking drunkenly): Oh YES!
Prim Lady: And what was the happiest?
Niven: Without question it was the time I saw Patsy Hendren at Lord's coming out to bat for Middlesex on a September afternoon. Halfway to the wicket he flung his bat in the air, let out a piercing shriek and disappeared at a brisk trot into the pavilion!

Prim Lady: Why did he do that?

Niven: He had a sleeping wasp in his box.

Prim Lady (mystified): His box?

Niven: Yes. That's a sort of aluminium single-seater bra which batsmen wear between their legs to protect their spare parts.

Prim Lady: I see. Now let's talk about your two little girls . . .

Jilly Cooper

Ladies and gentlemen, we have returned to the world of acting – Niven was a wonderful comic actor. A man with a similarly debonair style on stage was Rex Harrison, though few found him easy in private. Yet he could inspire huge affection in those he knew, and the theatre director Patrick Garland was one of them. For outsiders this is difficult to understand. Harrison was clearly a rogue, a bounder, a cad and a fiend.

Such men – and they are nearly always men – are like that. I was enormously fond of Randolph Churchill who was, on paper, even more ghastly than Harrison. (Remember that earlier bon mot of Evelyn Waugh's!) Yet you couldn't help loving him and he inspired wonderful stories. I remember when, as a callow youth, I auditioned for a job with Randolph and he asked me if I was any relation of the then famous Tory politician Sir Lionel Heald. I replied that, sadly, as far as I knew I was not. Randolph, unlike most people confronted with this disappointing news, did not look in the least downcast. Grinding out his cigarette and polishing off his Scotch he led me to the dining-room where a large and distinguished company were already waiting. Randolph looked round the throng with a gleam in his eye, banged his glass on the table and by way of grace thundered out, 'I have good news for you all. Our young friend here is no relation of Sir Lionel Heald.'

That could almost have been a Rex Harrison story, as Patrick Garland here implies in his affectionate tribute, given at the Garrick Club, to an awful old friend.

The incomparable Rex Harrison

Rex Harrison – so his wife, Elizabeth, told me, and she should know – was the only man who regularly sent back the wine in his own house. Elizabeth had survived two turbulent marriages, first to Richard Harris, and later to Rex Harrison. 'I was always deeply devoted to Rex', she said, '*before* we were married and *after* we were divorced. It was that little bit in between which proved so difficult.' When they were recently married, Rex had taken her to his house in Portofino (of which he was intensely fond) and was determined to do things in great style. Both were in evening dress for dinner, the view of the Mediterranean as the sun set was radiant, the setting was perfect. But everything went wrong. The hors d'oeuvres arrived soggy, warm red wine came up

with the fish, sour white wine accompanied the meat which was overcooked, and the Italian servants contrived to make a hash of all the carefully rehearsed arrangements. Rex flew into one of his characteristic rages. 'I've lived in the country for fifteen years,' he fumed. 'You would have thought the buggers would have learned to speak English by now . . .'

His relations with the local Italians were never particu-larly peaceful. The house was perched on the top of the hill, and an American film producer described to me how Rex instructed him to keep his head beneath the dashboard of the Jeep he used to fetch vegetables and visitors when he descended to the little sea-port, as the disaffected Italian butler peppered the vehicle with his shotgun. Another time, arriving at Rome with his customary excess baggage, there was a row with a local customs-officer, which ended with Rex screaming at him: 'Take your hat off when you're talking to me, you buffino!' Insulting an employee of the Italian state, when in uniform, is a prison offence, and to prevent a prosecution being carried out, formal apologies had to be made from the highest orders of the British Diplomatic Service.

Rex frequently referred to his six wives in terms both the-atrical and historical, and spoke of the beautiful Elizabeth Rhys-Williams, later Harris and later still Harrison, as 'the Katherine Howard part'. When Elizabeth and Rex were just married, Dulcie Gray told me, she went up to congratulate her, and told her that she was certain, after so many misfires, that Rex had finally found someone who would make him very happy.

'I think so too,' replied Elizabeth, 'and the first thing I'm going to do is get rid of that horrid little house in Portofino.' 'After that,' admitted Dulcie, 'I wasn't quite so confident.' Sometimes, not surprisingly, Rex got muddled as to whom he was married to, and once – after a row – when the beautiful and elegant Lilli Palmer stormed down the stairs and out of the front garden, Rex rushed after her shouting 'Come back . . . *you*!' When I was directing the revival of *My Fair Lady* in 1980, the legendary lyricist, Alan J. Lerner, at that time on wife number eight, joined Rex in a taxi to leave for the airport. The producer standing next to me murmured: 'Do you realise, Patrick, there are fourteen wives in that taxi . . .'

Throughout the explosive years of our association and, yes, friendship (at his Memorial Service, his widow, Mercia, told me, 'You know, Patrick, Rex *quite* liked you'), I often received wonderfully abusive postcards. There was one from Australia, where he was on tour with a Freddie Lonsdale comedy, with pictures of curious Antipodean marsupials, koalas, wombats, kangaroos, platypi, all looking extremely odd. 'You think these are peculiar,' he had scrawled, 'wait until you see the people.' And, when he was playing Lord Loam in *The Admirable Crichton*, he scribbled: 'I'm getting a little tired of playing the lovable old codge.' I confess, of all his personae, 'lovable old codge' was the least likely in my view, but I suppose none of us see ourselves unfavourably, or even, in Rex's case, remotely as we are.

The truth is he was as curmudgeonly and tyrannical to his fellow actors, directors and producers as he was to his former wives. But his particular *bêtes noires* were conductors. Rex was intolerant of many things and people and had a fine line in invective. He referred to the work of the geniuses who wrote *Gigi*, *My Fair Lady* and *Camelot* as Fritzy Loewe's 'contemptible tunes' and Alan Lerner's 'filthy lyrics'; living in the same New York apartment block as the retired screen goddess, Greta Garbo, he described her as 'a bad-tempered old bitch', and on one occasion, at a party she gave with guests as distinguished as Lilian Hellman, Leonard Bernstein, Henry Kissinger and Gore Vidal, when I expressed signs of awe and wonder, he dismissed them all as 'a frightful crew of drunks and deadbeats!' No flatterer of persons, he. But it was still conductors who drew his darkest rage, complaining in his favourite phrase: 'They set my teeth

on edge.' Of them all, the conductor who set his teeth on edge the most, unjustly in my view, was the excellent Franz Allers, who on occasion led the Vienna State Orchestra in Mahler and Strauss, and came out of retirement to conduct *My Fair Lady*, particularly in honour of Rex. When I told him of this benevolence, all Rex could find to say was: 'I don't like the look of that Nazi in the pit.' He always maintained, whatever hour of the day or night, Franz Allers 'invariably had the baton in his right hand, even at lunch', which was, I suppose, more or less the case. Franz was a martinet and I think somehow Rex envied this, and resented him as an acknowledged master of his craft. The end of 'I'm an Ordinary Man', which changes gear radically into the syncopated 'Let a Woman in Your Life', would challenge most people, Rex in particular, and Franz was agonised whenever it went wrong, which in rehearsals it did. 'If you would only look in my direction, my dear Rex,' he would plead in his tortured Anglo-Viennese accent, 'I am standing here with the baton, and as the tempo changes, you can follow me' – '*I* don't follow the conductor,' Rex would snarl, 'the conductor follows *me*.' Sometimes I wondered what might have happened if Rex had been conducted by Thomas Beecham. What was it he confided to his principal violinist when he put down his baton after conducting the Ballets Russes in *Swan Lake*? 'That made the buggers hop!'

The only conductor Rex ever admitted he admired was Cyril Ornadel, who, he declared, 'invented the conductor's crouch', a phrase entirely new to me. When I queried what he meant, Rex swiftly slackened his knees, bent his body forward, extended his arms but lowered his head beneath them, not unlike a swimmer about to dive into a swimming pool. The effect was to lower the conductor's head well below the parapet of the orchestra-pit so he was virtually invisible to the audience, or 'customers' as Rex called them. The explanation, after all, was blindingly simple. Rex could not bear anyone sharing the limelight, least of all in the musical department. He preferred altogether the associate-conductor, an excellent technician, but a far more modest personality, Bob Kriese. He was accustomed to call into the great man's dressing-room after every performance to see if there were any notes or criticisms, and would join me and a handful of the prettiest chorus girls for a relaxed chat and a glass of the very best white wine – 'No, Bob, nothing to say at all,' Rex would confirm, 'I feel absolutely safe in your hands.' 'Well, good night Mr Harrison . . .' said Bob, turning towards the door. 'Oh Bob, there is one thing as a matter of fact. Don't wear a tail-coat.' 'But Mr Harrison, of course I wear a tail-coat, in your honour, how could I not wear a tail-coat, it's unthinkable.'

'I know my dear fellow, but that's the problem. All that white means I can *see* you.'

It was the faithful Bob Kriese who was responsible for what I thought was one of the funniest Rexisms of the *My Fair Lady* tour. When we approached Chicago, Bob promised Rex the show would have the best pit-band in the

country, because they were all veterans of the old speakeasy days, and had played with Dizzy Gillespie, Mez Mezzrow, Bix Beiderbecke and his Chicagoans. Rex was very knowledgeable about the jazz of that era, having haunted Harlem in its great days of Duke Ellington and the Rainbow Room and the Apollo, so he was suitably enthusiastic for once.

'You'll love it, Rex, in Chicago,' reiterated Bob, 'they have this bright, brassy sound.' Even Rex picked up the refrain, and told me of the happy times we could look forward to in Chicago, because of its celebrated 'bright, brassy sound'. It became a kind of catch-phrase with the entire company.

When the day of the sitz-probe came around – that usually magical moment between cast and orchestra when they make music together for the first time after days of the rehearsal piano – Rex decided to give a speech of welcome. He stood above the twenty-six or so expectant musicians as they sat looking up at him, sunk as they were at the bottom of the pit:

'Ladies and gentlemen of the orchestra, it gives me the greatest pleasure to be here representing the *My Fair Lady* company which has enjoyed such splendid success playing your appreciative regional cities. Now we have finally arrived at Chicago, where the associate-conductor, Bob Kriese, assures me you are going to contribute a "bright, brassy sound" – of which, I trust, we will hear very little, as, to my experienced ear, I understand our composer, Mr Fritz Loewe, has composed a romantic all-string score.' Which was, of course, absolutely correct. To this day, I shall never forget the astonished but soundless gasp which greeted Rex's tactfully directed hand-grenade, and the row of stunned, upturned faces clutching the curved handles of their fiddles. With a respectful bow of his head, Rex turned lightly on his heel, and elegantly made his way upstage, towards his dressing-room. I followed meekly, and a few moments later he commented, enthusiastically: 'I think my little speech went down rather well with the musicians, didn't you, Patrick?'

One morning I received a telephone call from Doug Hayward, the excellent Gentleman's Tailor, who had often kitted out Rex in what he called his togs. 'It's Rex's birthday next month, and a group of us want to invite all his friends round to celebrate. So we've hired a telephone-booth.' This may well sound harsh, and it is true that, with so many casualties among his professional colleagues apart from his wives, agents, conductors, directors, producers, and other walking-wounded, there were not unbounded regiments of friends, but to imply there were none is a falsehood. Those who were fond of him were perhaps fairly few, but they remained very fond. I am among them. He has been dead for more than a decade now, but whenever there is a gathering of those associated with the 'Fair Lady' revival of 1980–81, we find we talk of nothing *but* Rex the entire evening. In fact, having worked with him is something of a genuine bond with others, rather like having retreated at Dunkirk, or battled at Monte Cassino. Two reasons, I think: first, that as a high comedian (of which I have said nothing) he was unequalled, and secondly, he was so deeply funny – even at his worst, even if you were on the receiving end.

John Cleese, in conversation with David Frost, trying to

account for the universal success of Basil Fawlty, explained that, contrary to the obvious view, rampant egocentricity is gloriously, joyfully funny – even, at times, hilarious. Rex Harrison lived a life of total selfishness, and aforementioned egocentricity. He died as selfishly and courageously and consistently as he lived. Warned that he might not recover from an operation (his liver turned out to be cancerous), he made it clear to the beautiful and final Mrs Harrison that he didn't want to hear the prognosis of the physicians, and he returned home, ashen-faced, shorn of hair-piece, false-teeth, sunken-cheeked and reedy-voiced. He resembled, in an unusual way, an exhausted and dying music-hall comedian, the kind of ancient character man who might emerge from the lower ranks of Vincent Crummles' company. Wife Mercia, sons Carey and Noël sat around in vigil. Perhaps unwisely, Carey leant over to his father, and called to him: 'I'm just going to step outside, Father, Mercia and Noël are here with you; is there anything I can do for you?' Almost immediately the sightless eyes opened, and the thin pipish trebles adopted their familiar rasp:

'Yes,' barked out Rex, 'drop dead! That's what you can do for me.' And beckoning his younger son to approach a little closer, muttered, 'Noël, there was something I always wanted to tell you. I could never stand the sound of your guitar.' And he died.

Patrick Garland

Rex Harrison was not the only actor to sail into battle against musicians. Dame Edith Evans also had a famous run-in with 'the band' while working with Peter Ustinov on a production of Sheridan's *The Rivals* during the war. The performances were to take place at the Garrison Theatre in Salisbury, and Ustinov was initially thrilled to be offered the service of a small orchestra, drawn from former members of the Berlin and Vienna Philharmonic orchestras. While they were united in their hatred of Hitler, the two orchestras also hated each other, and the rift between them was only healed when Dame Edith chose to remind them that this was not an opera with dialogue but a play with accompanying music. From then on they were united against 'zis woman', and Ustinov noted with some alarm that they were whiling away the spoken scenes by conducting a Berlin versus Vienna chess match. As all Ustinov's best stories are essentially after-dinner ones, I make no apology for including it here.

A run-in with Dame Edith Evans

I hoped to God Edith wouldn't notice this. She was wonderful on the first night and got great applause. On the second night in mid-speech she stopped dead. She saw the chessboard, and because she was an actress of great experience she turned to me and said, 'What did you say?'

I invented some Sheridan, 'Madam, though the humours of Bath be but a diversion to our contumely, I will not pre-sume on your generosity to the extent of belittling those very qualities which, while they look to us but scant justice before the evil tongues of the town, nevertheless becalm the odious and bring success to fools.'

She, not unnaturally, said, 'What!?'

We gradually pushed each other off the stage, and she exclaimed, 'It's a Gilbertian situation. I can't have them playing chess.'

So I went to Dr Strietzel afterwards and began by saying, 'It was better tonight.'

'You noticed, you are a real musician. You noticed the Boccherini was good for the first time. These people from Vienna, they have such a soft touch.'

'Yes, that was better, but there's one thing I complain about.'

'Yes please, ve are open to criticisms.'

'Is it really necessary to play chess on a miniature board?'

'It disturbs you?'

'Yes.'

'No, that's not true. You it doesn't disturb, because you are a real actor. It disturbs zis woman.'

'She is a very famous actress and a very good person.'

'Ve don't see zis, and it's only a very little board.'

'It makes it worse because you have to reach further.'

'All right. If you say ve can't play chess, ve don't play chess.'

He walked out and I dreaded the future. I was right, because at the next performance Edith didn't get any laughs at all. She couldn't concentrate, she was all over the place. When I went on the stage I saw exactly what had happened. They had abandoned the chess, but had now arranged themselves in a long line facing us and lit from underneath. They looked like the dock at Nuremberg. Their eyes followed Edith wherever she went. Afterwards I went up to Dr Strietzel and said, 'Look, this won't do.'

'So, tell me if I'm wrong, no? First it was the chessboard, ve shouldn't play chess. Why? The woman doesn't like it. Now, ve can't even watch her, you think it gives us pleasure to watch her? Ve who have seen Paula Wessely at her great-est!?'

I said, 'No, that doesn't enter into it. It's very, very unpleasant this, I felt you watching us all the time.'

'You ve weren't watching, ve know you. Ve were watching her!'

I made them promise to stop. The next night she didn't get any laughs at all, though I couldn't see why not. There were a lot of generals in, but I didn't think they could be as dim as all that. So when I was off stage I ripped round to the back of the auditorium, and the musicians had turned them-selves with their backs to the stage, still lit from underneath, but now just staring at the audience. I can only tell you they went back to their chess, and Edith never mentioned it again; because the one thing she couldn't bear was someone astride her lines of communication with the public.

Peter Ustinov

And finally, ladies and gentlemen, to me. Throughout this caper through the tangled briars and thickets that make up the world of the after-dinner speaker I have been more than normally aware that, for all those who bring off that difficult task with memorable wit, charm and panache, there are hundreds who fail. We have met a few of them in these pages. We have not yet made the acquaintance of Reg Brackett. Ladies and gentlemen – let us end with a caution-ary tale . . .

Business unusual or THE END

'Fellow members of the Scarpington Artisans' Lodge, Your Graces, My Lord, ladies and gentlemen . . .' Reg Brackett, MBE (for community services), picked nervously at his chain of office and flashed his dentures at the assembled company. One hundred and seventy-three souls were crammed into the King Alfred the Great Banqueting Room at the three-star Talbot Hotel, flagship of the Jolly Trencherman chain, owned by Scarpington's most successful son, Sir Seymour Puce, MP for the city, who was seated on the left of the Countess of Scarpington herself. Black-tied Artisans and their wives were augmented by the great and good of Scarpington and District. The Earl of Scarpington, Grand Patron of the Lodge, was guest of honour and would speak next. The Bishop of Scarpington had said the traditional Artisans' Grace ('For these thy gifts, the fruits of thy mercy and of our dutiful toil and labour, we thank thee, Lord') and they had all scoffed their way through the Fruit Cocktail Artisan, the Baron of Beef Scarpington and the Coupe Talbot.

Now the nose-powdering break was over, the port was on the table and this year's President of the Artisans was on his feet. It was not so much that Reg was unaccustomed to public speaking, more that he didn't seem to be able to get the hang of it. He had raided hundreds of Gyles Brandreth joke books, knew every Englishman, Scotsman, Irishman and Welshman story in the world and could even manage sexy racism – though he tended to keep that for stag nights. Despite this, or perhaps because of it, his after-dinner speeches were literally stunning.

All round the King Alfred Room men and women looked duly stunned. The strong drinks before dinner coupled with the Blue Nun and the Nuits-St-Georges had a lot to do with this, but so did Reg. As Chairman and Chief Executive of Bracketts Laundry and Dry Cleaning Services (Est. 1936) Reg was a force in the land. Had he not been a force in the land he would not, naturally, have been President of the Artisans. The Artisans of Scarpington were to the Masons or the Rotary as the Brigade of Guards to the Pioneer Corps. They were an élite. Of course Scarpington had its Round Table and its Guild of Scarpington Men, but they were as

New Zealand Cheddar to Stilton. Membership of the Scarpington Artisans' Lodge was what all good burghers of
Scarpington wished for themselves. To be an Artisan was to
have arrived. They were, paradoxically, the salt of Scarpington and its cream as well.

All along the top table sat the predecessors of President
Brackett. Brown of Brown's Dairy; Green of Green and
Green, Builders Merchants; Sinclair of Sinclair's who made
custom-built invalid carriages and had once held the war-
rant for the Royal House of Iraq; Festing of Festing,
Festing, Hackett, Festing and Festing, the top solicitors in
town; Moulton of Moulton and Bragg, the brewers of
Scarpington Special; Fothergill, owner and proprietor of the
Scarpington Times (incorporating the *Scarpington Clarion
and Farringay Echo*).

They were all there with their wives; all plump with dinner and self-importance; all nodding off quietly almost in
time to Brackett's post-prandial drone.

As the speech wore on, it seemed to those very few who
were paying attention that Reg's speech was becoming
more than usually slurred and his delivery more than usually
faltering. He told the story about the Englishman, the
Scotsman and the Irishman on the desert island with even
less than his customary panache.

'So the Englishman says to the genie, "Take me back to
Blighty"; and the genie claps his hands and the Englishman
vanishes.' The Earl of Scarpington's head fell on to his chest
and he breathed very heavily for a moment before shaking
himself awake like an ancient Sealyham coming in from the
rain. 'And the Scotsman says to the genie, "Take me back to
Glasgie"; and the genie claps his hands and the Scotsman
vanishes.'

Brown glanced at Green and winked; Fothergill looked
at Festing and raised an eyebrow; Sinclair stifled a yawn.
Reg Brackett's voice was beginning to sound like an old
gramophone record fast running down.

'And finally,' he said, 'the genie asks the Irishman for his wish and the Irishman says . . .'

Almost everyone present had heard Reg tell the story at the Scarpington Scarecrows Cricket Club Annual Dinner and Dance in this very room less than a month earlier, so they all knew what the Irishman's wish was. But this time the wish was never articulated for just as Reg was about to tell everyone what it was his eyes, which had almost shut, suddenly opened very wide and revolved briefly. There was a momentary gargling sound and he fell forward with startling rapidity, smashing a port glass with his forehead and ending face down on the table where he lay quite still.

He was, of course, extremely dead.

Tim Heald

Acknowledgements

Every effort has been made to contact copyright holders; in the event of an inadvertent omission or error, the editorial department should be notified at The Folio Society Ltd, 44 Eagle Street, London, WC1R 4FS.

The Folio Society wishes to thank the following writers, publishers and literary representatives for their permission to use copyright material:

Baldwin, Stanley: 'On England' and 'Advice on speech-making' reproduced by permission of the Earl Baldwin of Bewdley.

Baring, Maurice: 'Such a treat' from C (Heinemann, 1934) reproduced by permission of the Trustees of the Maurice Baring Wills Trust and House of Stratus Ltd.

Beaverbrook, Lord: 'Apprentice', 25 May 1964, reproduced by permission of The Beaverbrook Foundation.

Brandreth, Gyles: 'Gobbledegook or small print' copyright © Gyles Brandreth, 1992.

Braun, Thomas: 'A birthday tribute to Jasper Griffin' from a speech given at Jasper Griffin's birthday luncheon, 8 June 1997, © Thomas Braun, 1997.

Burnett, David: 'To the Society of Dorset Men', 27 October 2001, copyright © David Burnett, 2001.

Chesterton, G. K.: 'Speechlessness' from a speech given at the 60th birthday dinner of Hilaire Belloc, 1930, reproduced by permission of A. P. Watt Ltd on behalf of The Royal Literary Fund.

Churchill, Winston: 'To the Corinthians', 24 January 1904, copyright © Winston Churchill, reproduced by permission of Curtis Brown on behalf of the Estate of Winston Churchill.

Cooper, Jilly: 'Meeting David Niven' from a personal letter dated 11 July 2002, copyright © Jilly Cooper 2002.

Davies, Robertson: 'Refuge of insulted saints' from *High Spirits* by Robertson Davies, copyright © 1982 by Robertson Davies. Used by permission of Viking Penguin, a division of Penguin Group (USA) Inc.

Edinburgh, Duke of: 'To the French Chamber of Commerce', 9 May 1963, copyright © HRH Duke of Edinburgh, 1963.

Elizabeth II, Queen: 'Golden wedding' – speech made at the Banqueting House luncheon, 20 November 1997, copyright © HRH Queen Elizabeth II, 1997.

Fielding, Helen: 'Bridget Jones at a wedding' from *Bridget Jones: The Edge of Reason* (Picador, 1999) copyright © Helen Fielding, 1999, reproduced by permission of PanMacmillan and Gillon Aitken Associates.

Fothergill, John: 'Falls of Lodore' from *An Innkeeper's Diary* (Chatto and Windus, 1931) reproduced by permission of Jane Fothergill and John Fothergill.

Garland, Patrick: 'Lord David Cecil's dismay' from 'A man whose disapproval one would least like to have', and 'The Incomparable Rex Harrison', reproduced by permission of Patrick Garland.

Grenfell, Joyce: 'Useful and acceptable gifts' from *Stately as a Galleon* (Macmillan, 1978) copyright © Joyce Grenfell, 1978, reproduced by permission of Sheil Land Associates on behalf of J G Productions.

Heald, Tim: 'Business unusual or THE END' from *Business Unusual* (Macmillan, 1986) © Tim Heald, 1986.

Heald, Tim: 'An Evening with Brian Johnston' from *Brian Johnston: The Authorised Biography* (Methuen, 1995) © Tim Heald, 1995.

Herbert, A. P.: 'Winston Churchill', 'The English laugh', 'The English laugh – again' and 'The English laugh – chorus' from the English Association Presidential Address (Oxford University Press, 1950) © The English Association, reproduced by permission of The English Association.

Herbert, A. P.: 'After dinner' reproduced by permission of A. P. Watt on behalf of Jocelyn Hale and Teresa Elizabeth Perkins.

Hoffnung, Gerard: 'From a bricklayer in Golders Green', Oxford Union, 4 December 1958, reproduced by permission of Anita Hoffnung.

Holroyd, Michael: 'A prominent feature' copyright © Michael Holroyd.

Ind, William, Bishop of Truro: 'Not enough cricket' – speech to the XL Club Dinner, 19 October 2001, copyright © The Bishop of Truro 2001.